Where to Join

A Guide for Young People

Where to Join

A Guide for Young People

Helen Pain

Department of Library & Information Studies
Loughborough University of Technology

Northcote House

Acknowledgements

The author is grateful for the kind assistance provided by the various organisations in the preparation of this book.

First published in 1988 by Northcote House Publishers Ltd, Harper & Row House, Estover Road, Plymouth PL6 7PZ, United Kingdom.
Tel: Plymouth (0752) 705251. Telex: 45635. Fax: (0752) 777603.

Note: We regret that the author's biographical details have been incorrectly given on the back cover. Helen Pain is Editor of the School Libraries Group of the Library Association.

British Library Cataloguing in Publication Data

Pain, Helen
Where to join : a guide for young people.
1. Youth – Great Britain – Recreation – Handbooks, manuals, etc.
I. Title
790.1'92 GV75

ISBN 0-7463-0378-5

Printed in Great Britain by A. Wheaton & Co. Ltd., Exeter

Contents

CONTENTS

What this Book is About

Ever feel bored? At a loose end? I know that I did when I was your age. Well, from now on there is no need for you to feel like this again, because you have discovered *Where to Join*!

What is *Where to Join?*

It is a book specially written for young people from nine to sixteen years old. It aims to give ideas of things to do in your leisure time – hobbies and sports to start, and clubs, societies and associations to join. There are even pressure groups included which you can join and so play a part in making the world a better place to live in.

How was it put together?

When asked to write this book, the first thing I did was to talk to young people, and to adults who work with young people, asking them what hobbies and sports they would like to see included. The *Directory of British Associations* then provided me with names and addresses of clubs, societies and associations to write to for information. Many of these replied to me with lots of information for which I thank them. However, not all replied. Sometimes I have been able to get a little information from elsewhere about some of these organisations; others, unfortunately, have had to be left out. Also, some hobbies have no club or society which accepts young people as members, so you may not find your hobby here for this reason. Why not start your own club with a few friends?

On page 167 you will find a section headed **More Useful Addresses.** This gives the addresses of some organisations for which more detailed information is not yet available. I hope, when this book appears in a second edition, it will be possible to include more national clubs, societies and associations. Why not write and tell me if you know about any that are not yet in the book? You will find a form for this on page 169.

How do I use it?

The book is arranged by interest: for example, birds, circuses, football, railways, thimble collecting and so on. The Contents list shows all the interests you will find covered in this book. Under each interest heading there are listed the names of clubs, societies and associations with short descriptions of what they do. You can join these yourself, or perhaps get your club or school to join them. Or, if they are associations which only clubs join, they will be able to tell you where your local club meets. In all cases you will find that knowing about the organisation will help you to enjoy your hobby or sport much more, and may even suggest a new interest for you to follow. Under each entry you will find a quick reference section telling you who to apply to for further information, what age groups between nine and sixteen can join, how many members there are, and when the organisation started. There is also a guide to how much it is to join and what the subscription is each year. This guide is coded as follows:

A	free to about £2.00
B	£2 to about £6.00
C	£6 to about £11.00
D	£11 to about £15

There is also an index which should *always* be used, because some organisations cover more than one interest, but appear only once in the book. The index at the back of the book will lead you to these. It also lists the names of all the organisations included.

You will find pages in the book on which you can jot down your own ideas and notes. Also, on page 38 you will find a sample letter which you can copy if you want to write to one of the national organisations about joining. On page 150 there is another letter to copy if you want to write to a national organisation to find out if there is a local club you can join.

Is that all I need to know?

No. As well as using this book, remember that some schools and public libraries keep files of the names and addresses of local clubs and societies, and will be very pleased to help you. Also, if you write to the addresses in this book you might be unlucky and have your letter returned and marked 'gone away'. It is hoped that this will not happen, but clubs, societies and associations do sometimes move. If this does happen, do not despair; your public library may be able to do some detective work for you and come up with a new address, as well as tell you about local clubs.

Finally, let me wish you an exciting time when following up your interests, meeting new friends and developing your skills and knowledge. This book aims to bring pleasure, and I hope that it will for you.

Have fun,

Helen Pain

1

The Arts

Central Council of Church Bell-Ringers

19 Ravensgate Road
Charlton Kings
Cheltenham
Gloucestershire GL53 8NR
Tel: (0242) 32454

Change ringing means ringing church tower bells to methods of numbers.These are not well-known tunes, but have their own patterns and are very fascinating to learn. Change ringing of church tower bells is organised in the British Isles by the Central Council of Church Bell-Ringers which is the controlling committee for all guilds and associations of ringers.

Church towers with five or more ringable bells will often have a local band of ringers who are always glad to teach learners. You can find out the name of the Tower Captain by asking at the church or simply going along when you hear the bells ringing on a weekday evening. Look for a small door in the corner of the tower if you cannot see the ringers, and climb the spiral staircase.

Practice nights are usually once a week between 7.00 pm and 9.00 pm. Once you have learned to ring you will be able to ring for Sunday services and weddings. Each tower has its own practice night which does not change.

Most ringers belong to their local guild or association and pay a subscription to that, as well as to their own tower. The amount varies according to the association but is rarely more than two or three pounds for the year for both together.

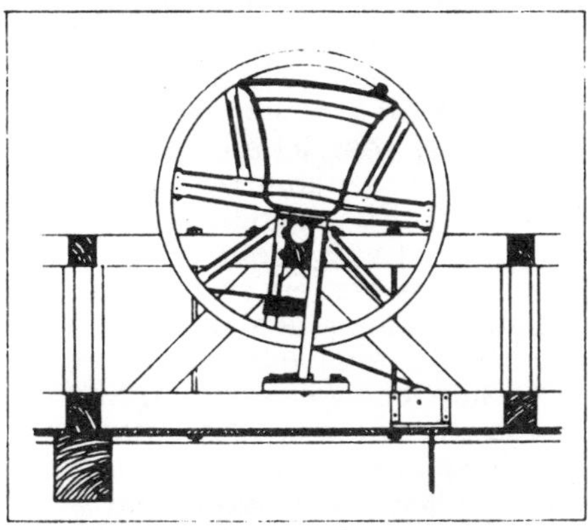

The weekly journal of church bell-ringers is *The Ringing World.* It costs 55p and can be ordered through a newsagent or directly by post from *The Ringing World,* Penmark House, Woodbridge Meadows, Guildford GU1 1BL.

Apply to	the address above, for further information
Age range	10–16
Joining fee	none
Annual fee	varies with local group of ringers
Members	99
Date started	1891

Handbell Ringers of Great Britain (HRGB)

2 Holt Park Approach
Leeds LS16 7PW
Tel: (0532) 677711

HRGB is the national organisation for the many teams of handbell ringers in Britain. Any handbell team can register with the HRGB; there are teams with as few as three members holding four bells each, to large bell orchestras ringing off tables. All styles of time ringing are included. However, an aspect of handbell ringing which HRGB does *not* cater for is the ringing of tower bell methods on handbells. Teams which do this tend to look more towards their local tower bell guild or society.

The HRGB organises a national rally every year, where handbell teams meet together to ring. Local rallies are organised by the seven regions of this Society, which also publish newsletters and keep in touch with their local teams. Advice is available to members, who also receive a six-monthly magazine called *Reverberations.* Music specially arranged for handbells is published by the HRGB for you to play and enjoy.

Write now and find out where your nearest team meets. You will be sure of a warm welcome.

Apply to	Mr Malcolm C. Wilson, 'Elmbank', Doune Rd, Dunblane, Perthshire FK15 9AR
Age range	9–16
Joining fee	none
Annual fee	A
Members	3,086
Date started	1967

Institute of Amateur Cinematographers (IAC)

63 Woodfield Lane
Ashtead
Surrey KT21 2BT
Tel: (03722) 76358

Whether you film with single, standard or super 8, 9.5, 16 mm or video; whether you specialise in historical epics in widescreen or 'baby on the lawn' footage; whether you are a club member or not, film collector or movie buff, there is a warm welcome awaiting you from the IAC and its members.

When you join you can take advantage of the experts on all cine matters, who are on hand to help you. No question is too simple or too hard. You can get advice on scripting, shooting, editing, sound, lighting, music, animation, presentation and technical matters. Every two months you will receive the *Amateur Film Maker*, full of news, reviews and previews of IAC activities, and articles on all aspects of film making. There is also a unique copyright clearance scheme for music and recordings used for film and video sound tracks and for tape/slide presentation. You can enter the IAC International Film Competition, which attracts entries from all over the world, and is very highly thought of.

Every member receives a membership card, which can help you in getting permission to film in places you might otherwise be refused access to, and a lapel badge.

Apply to	the address above
Age range	older readers
Joining fee	A
Annual fee	B
Members	2,750
Date started	1932

Mercia Cinema Society

West Dene
Manchester Road
Rochdale
Greater Manchester OL11 3PJ

This Society was started by a group of people who were concerned that cinemas were disappearing rapidly without any proper records being kept about them. Years ago there were 5,000 cinemas, and going to see films was a very popular way of spending your leisure time; today there are only about 700. All sorts of cinemas are of interest to this Society from fairground bioscope shows through penny gaffs, the very common fleapits, the 'super-cinemas' of the 1930s, to the present day 'multiplexes'.

The Society works at keeping the memory of the cinemas alive by producing fully-illustrated books about cinema history, holding occasional meetings and events (such as visits to cinemas), and arranging to preserve a cinema with the North of England Open Air Museum at Beamish in County Durham.

If you join this Society you will receive two magazines, *Mercia Bioscope* and *Mercia Newsreel* four times a year. *Mercia Bioscope* is fully-illustrated and features short historical articles about various cinemas and aspects of the cinema trade in the United Kingdom. *Mercia Newsreel* gives details about the current cinema scene in the United Kingdom, usually closures, but the occasional opening of a new cinema, too.

Apply to	Mr Charles Morris, at the address above
Age range	older readers
Joining fee	none
Annual fee	B
Members	162
Date started	1980

Circus Fans' Association of Great Britain (CFA)

43 Waterloo Lane
Skellingthorpe
Lincoln
Lincolnshire LN6 5SJ
Tel: (0522) 683272

Originally the word circus meant a Roman oval or circular structure, ringed with tiers of seats, in which spectacular entertainments were offered. Today's circus still offers spectacular entertainment, but this usually includes a variety of trained animal acts and exhibitions of human skill and daring. The circus as we know it began in England in 1768: Philip Astley, a trick rider, found that galloping his horse in a circle whilst standing on its back improved his balance. In doing so he traced the first ring. The name circus was first used in 1782 when the Royal Circus began.

The CFA is for all of you interested in any aspect of circuses. If you join you will be able to take part in special rallies to circuses where you can meet the artistes and see behind the scenes. Four times a year you will receive *King Pole*, a magazine full of photographs and features on circus stars past and present. You can also borrow from a collection of books on circuses, and the CFA will be pleased to answer any of your questions about circuses.

Apply to	the address above
Age range	9–16
Joining fee	none
Annual fee	C
Members	675
Date started	1934

British Ballet Organisation (BBO)

39 Lonsdale Road
London SW13 9JP
Tel: (01) 748 1241

If you go along to a ballet class you would join the BBO which provides ballet and stage dancing examinations for you to take. When a member, you will receive a newsletter three times a year, as well as have the chance to improve your ballet.

Apply to	the address above
Age range	must have passed the elementary examination
Joining fee	by taking examinations and paying fees coded C
Annual fee	none
Members	2,500
Date started	1930

English Folk Dance and Song Society (EFDSS)

Cecil Sharp House
2 Regent's Park Road
London NW1 7AY
Tel: (01) 485 2206

The EFDSS came about by the joining together of the Folk Song Society and the English Folk Dance Society. Its aim is to encourage the practice and enjoyment of folk music, dance, song, customs and drama.

Each year dances, concerts, ceilidhs and festivals are organised, including the world's largest folk festival. Singers, callers, bands, dancers and mummers are provided for many events throughout England. Training courses, workshops, lectures and classes are arranged so that members can learn more about English folk tradition.

If you join the EFDSS you will receive copies of the magazine

English Dance and Song, and the *Folk Music Journal*, and you can borrow books from the Vaughan Williams Memorial Library, and select from the books and records sold by the Society.

Apply to	the Membership Secretary, at the address above
Age range	11 – 16
Joining fee	none
Annual fee	B
Members	over 10,000
Date started	1932

Hobby Horse Club of England

38 Howick Cross Lane
Penwortham
Preston
Lancashire PR1 ONS

This Club is part of the English Folk Dance and Song Society, but is for young people interested in 'folk' who are under thirteen years old. There are local clubs throughout England, and by writing to the address above you can find out where your nearest club meets. These local clubs organise activities which include morris, clog and sword dancing, music, crafts, mummers' plays and social dance. There are also festivals and holidays in which you can take part.

By joining the Hobby Horse Club you can enjoy and learn about English music, dance and song traditions. You will also receive a newsletter, a birthday card and a member's badge.

Apply to	Alan Barber, Honorary Organiser, at the address above
Age range	9–13
Joining fee	none
Annual fee	A
Members	about 350
Date started	1981

The Morris Ring

50 Albert Road
Ledbury
Herefordshire HR8 2DW
Tel: (0531) 2765

The Morris dance has a very ancient history. Today in its various forms it is greatly enjoyed by those who dance and those who watch it. If you would like to learn how to take part in this traditional dance then The Morris Ring will be able to tell you where your local club can be found. These clubs are members of the Ring, and receive, two or three times a year, *The Morris Ring Circular* full of interesting news, letters and entertaining articles. Several clubs have their own junior sides.

Joining a Morris dance club can not only give you a lot of fun, but also help you to keep a part of our cultural tradition alive.

Apply to	Mr Keith Francis, at the address above
Age range	9–16
Joining fee	none
Annual fee	paid by local clubs
Members	170 clubs
Date started	1934

Drama Association of Wales (DAW)

Chapter Arts Centre
Canton
Cardiff CF5 1QE
Tel: (0222) 43794

If you live in Wales and enjoy going to see amateur dramatics, or are involved in an amateur dramatics group, then the DAW may well be of interest to you.

Through joining you will receive *DAW News* four times a year, which keeps you in touch with amateur theatre throughout Wales. Theatre groups can benefit from visits by advisers to discuss local problems and seek ways for the Association to help. Stage lanterns, stage drapes and other equipment can be hired from DAW at very reasonable prices. Grants are available to help with training activities, special productions, forming new groups and temporary financial difficulties. The DAW's staff offer advice and information on all aspects of the theatre; copies of plays and sound effects and dialect recordings may be borrowed for a small fee from the Association's library. In addition, DAW organises a national conference, a one-act play festival, a playwrighting competition followed by a weekend school for playwrights, and a week-long residential summer school.

Apply to	Mr R.R. Haddon, the Director, at the address above
Age range	older readers
Joining fee	none
Annual fee	B
Members	306
Date started	1965

National Drama Festivals Association (NDFA)

24 Jubilee Road
Formby
Liverpool L37 2HT
Tel: (07048) 72421

Interested in going to see amateur dramatics and drama festivals? If so, join the NDFA and be kept informed about when and where festivals are being held. As a member you will receive, each year, a Directory giving full information about all festivals organised by members. Four times a year a *Festival Newsletter* will be delivered to you, giving you up-to-date details of festival programmes and results, plus news from members and information received from other drama organisations.

Apply to	Brenda Nicholl, Honorary Secretary at the address above
Age range	older readers
Joining fee	none
Annual fee	B
Members	82
Date started	1964

Scottish Community Drama Association (SCDA)

Saltire House
13 Atholl Crescent
Edinburgh EH3 8HG
Tel: (031) 229 7838

This Association encourages amateur drama in Scotland, and welcomes drama clubs, schools and anyone who is interested in its work. If you join SCDA you will be able to take part in competitive festivals for one-act and full-length plays, training courses and summer schools, youth theatre work, playwrighting competitions, and international exchange between drama clubs, all organised by the Association. Also available to members are five libraries of play scripts and books on drama, and a staff of professional drama tutors and producers who will travel anywhere in Scotland.

Four times a year you will receive its magazine *Scene*.

Apply to	the address above
Age range	older readers
Joining fee	none
Annual fee	C
Members	1,350
Date started	1926

Young Theatre Association (YTA)

British Theatre Association
Darwin Infill Building
Regent's College
London NW1
Tel: (01) 387 2666

When you join the YTA you can attend a number of courses including Saturday morning workshops, Sunday production groups, weekend courses, four day courses held each Christmas and Easter, and the one week YTA summer school. Also, you receive, four times a year, *Drama Magazine*, and can get information about drama activities in your local area. Your membership card can be used at certain theatres to buy tickets at student standby prices.

Apply to	Chris Banfield, at the address above
Age range	12–16
Joining fee	none
Annual fee	C
Members	400
Date started	1954

The British Federation of Music Festivals

Festivals House
198 Park Lane
Macclesfield
Cheshire SK11 6UD
Tel: (0625) 28297

Competitive music festivals play an important role in keeping alive local interest in the arts, and also can provide a great deal of enjoyment for those taking part or in the audience. There are 300 competitive festivals, held in country towns, busy cities, or village communities — in fact wherever there is an interest in the arts. If you enjoy joining in music festivals, then the Federation's Year-book, containing lists of festivals and their dates, will be very useful to you. It can be bought for £3.50 from the Federation.

Apply to	the Secretary at the address above
Age range	9–16
Joining fee	none
Annual fee	none
Date started	1921

British Flute Society (BFS)

65 Marlborough Place
London NW8 OPT

The BFS organises recitals, master classes and lectures by famous flautists. James Galway, John Francis and Jean Pierre Rampal have conducted master classes, and William Bennett, Peter Lucas Graf, Stephen Preston, Ray Swingfield and Trevor Wye are amongst the well-known performers who have played at meetings in London, Manchester and Birmingham.

If you join the BFS you will be invited to these, and will receive four times a year *Pan*, a magazine full of reviews and articles on flutes, flautists, flute-playing and music. Through this magazine's small ad and letter columns you can get to know other flautists in your area, buy and sell second-hand flutes and music, and obtain information.

Apply to	the Secretary, at the address above
Age range	9–16
Joining fee	none
Annual fee	C
Members	1,210
Date started	1983

British Music Society (BMS)

40 Laburnham Road
Maidenhead
Berkshire SL6 4DE
Tel: (0628) 29505

The BMS encourages people to listen to the music of British composers, especially those composers no longer alive and who have been responsible for writing some very good music.

When you join the BMS you will receive a journal once a year which includes articles on British composers such as Arthur Bliss, John Rayner, Christopher Headington, William Wordsworth, and Rebecca Clarke. Four times a year a free newsletter is sent to you, telling you about forthcoming events, and including reviews of records, books and live music. The Society also publishes *British Composer Profiles*, a biographical dictionary and chronology of British composers 1800 – 1979, and helps with the production of cassettes and records. All of these you can buy at special lower prices. Concerts and lectures are also arranged.

Apply to	the Honorary Secretary at the address above
Age range	older readers
Joining fee	none
Annual fee	B
Members	370
Date started	1978

Hallé Concerts Society (Hallé)

30 Cross Street
Manchester M2 7BA
Tel: (061) 834 8363

If you live within easy travelling distance of Manchester, enjoy music, and would like to help support an orchestra, then join this Society. The Hallé Concerts Society exists to maintain the famous Hallé Orchestra, and to organise and present orchestral concerts. When you join the Hallé you get priority booking for two season tickets, and for two single tickets for each public concert in Manchester, as well as being able to reserve a season ticket from season to season. You also receive copies of the *Annual Prospectus* and *Proms Prospectus* each year, which tell you about forthcoming concerts, and you can even get a rehearsal pass to see the orchestra preparing for a concert.

Apply to	the Secretary, at the address above
Age range	9–16
Joining fee	none
Annual fee	B
Members	5,128
Date started	1899

National Accordion Organisation of Great Britain (NAO)

PO Box 91
Warrington WA1 1SY
Tel: (061) 7757695

Members of NAO include players and enthusiasts in all parts of Britain. When you join you can seek information and solutions to problems from the experienced staff, and keep in touch with accordion activities in Britain and abroad through the magazine *The Accordionist*, sent to you eight times a year.

Area festivals are held throughout Britain between September and February each year, and you can enter these at a lower fee. There is also a final All-British Championship each year, usually in April or May. The winners of the Virtuoso Championship are awarded a special twelve month scholarship to train under the most suitable and highly respected professors of music.

Apply to	Mr K.G. Farran, at the address above
Age range	9–16
Joining fee	none
Annual fee	B
Members	1,028
Date started	1947

NAO

National School Band Association (NSBA)

'Eastcliff'
Side Cliff Road
Roker
Sunderland SR6 9PX
Tel: (0783) 487193

NSBA aims to encourage the development of brass bands in schools. When you join you will be able to go to lectures, and courses held all over Britain on a local and national basis. Most of these are residential, providing opportunities for discussion as well as conducting, playing, and other activities involved in performing in ensembles.

Local festivals and inter-school visits take place throughout Britain. One or more national festivals at both junior and senior levels are organised each year, and finish with a concert of pieces played by massed bands under a guest conductor. These are purely music-making occasions, to provide pleasure and improve the general standard of performance; this has become so high that

several festivals have been broadcast on radio and television. A large amount of music has been specially written for the NSBA, and given its first performance during these annual festivals.

You will receive the magazine *Trumpeter* each term, providing news and reviews of new music. Membership is open to any school brass or wind band, any brass or wind bands of youth organisations, or anyone interested in brass band music and the work of the NSBA.

Apply to	Mr A. Winwood, Secretary, at the address above
Age range	9–16
Joining fee	none
Annual fee	B - individual membership; C - school band membership
Members	240
Date started	1952

Pipers' Guild

11 Lambourn Way
Tunbridge Wells
Kent TN2 5HJ
Tel: (0892) 36714

There are branches of this Guild all over Britain, and their members are interested in making, decorating and playing bamboo pipes. There are branch meetings, evening classes, weekend courses and gatherings and summer schools. To be a full member of the Guild, you must have made a pipe yourself, although you can join as an associate member if you just want to support its aims. However, if you want to make a pipe, you can learn at classes held in London and in several other places around the country, or at a special weekend school.

If you join, you get a newsletter twice a year telling you about the Guild's activities. Write now and find out more about this unusual hobby.

Apply to	Jake Jones, 15 St Michael's Road, Madeley, Telford, Shropshire
Age range	9–16
Joining Fee	none
Annual fee	B
Members	300
Date started	1932

Royal Scottish Pipe Band Association (RSPBA)

45 Washington Street
Glasgow G3 8AZ
Tel: (041) 221 5414

The RSPBA promotes pipe band music worldwide, organising competitions, examinations and meetings. It also provides an information service, so if you want to know more just write and ask; the Association's staff will be pleased to help.

Apply to	Mr Robert Nichol, at the address above
Age range	9–16
Joining fee	B
Annual fee	B associate membership
Members	22,000
Date started	1930

The Society of Recorder Players (SRP)

469 Merton Road
London SW18 5LD
Tel: (01) 874 2237

Players of recorders of all ages and all standards are welcomed by this Society, but it does not teach the recorder. However, it does provide people with the chance to play together, to get to know the wealth of recorder music available, and to experience the leadership of experienced conductors and musical directors.

One of the SRP's aims is to try and help those young people who played and enjoyed the recorder in junior school and who now want to continue, but have been forced to give it up at secondary school where it may not be part of the music curriculum.

Throughout Britain there are branches for you to join. Some of these have a scheme for the award of the Certificate of the Society; you receive this after an examination which tests what you know about recorders and their music, and the ability to play and to lead a recorder group. Each year the branch receives a visit from a national panel of conductors.

The SRP also organises annual national festivals with mass playing, competitions and concerts. Also, you are able to buy at a special lower price, a magazine *Recorder and Music*, published four times a year. To find out where your local branch meets, write now to the SRP.

Apply to	Mrs Anne Blackman, Honorary Secretary, at the address above
Age range	9–16
Joining fee	none
Annual fee	varies with the branch you join
Members	1,590
Date started	1937

British Federation of Young Choirs (BFYC)

Loughborough Technical College
Radmoor Road
Loughborough
Leicestershire LE11 3BT
Tel: (0509) 215831 extension 38

Are you interested in singing and choral music? This Federation offers its members, which include choirs, advice and information about musical events, repertoire, courses, funding, travel and exchanges, and other matters relating to choral singing. It also holds practical courses for singers and choirs throughout the year. The Federation is able to offer financial help to its members to enable them to attend a BFYC course, programme, seminar, or choral event organised by BFYC abroad, or any other special singing event or festival.

Apply to	Susan Lansdale or Muriel Blackwell at the address above
Age range	9–16
Joining fee	none
Annual fee	B
Members	202
Date started	1983

NOTES

2

Clubs

ARMED FORCES

Air Training Corps

The Public Relations Office
HQ Air Cadets
RAF Newton
Nottingham NG13 8HR
Tel: (0949) 20771 extension 441

The ATC aims to promote and encourage in young people (both boys and girls) a practical interest in aviation; it provides training which will be useful in civilian or Service life; and seeks to foster a spirit of adventure, to develop the qualities of leadership and good citizenship.

There are more than a thousand ATC Squadrons throughout Britain. In each average-sized Squadron there are around forty cadets. They meet on two evenings a week from 7.15 pm to 9.15 pm, and often there are weekend activities. If you join the ATC some of the things you could find yourself doing and learning about are aero-modelling, aircraft operation, air navigation, amateur radio, athletics, camping, canoeing, community relations, competition shooting, cross-country running, drill, the Duke of Edinburgh's Award Scheme, first aid, flying and gliding, map-reading, orienteering, overseas visits, photography, rock climbing, playing rugby, sailing, playing soccer, space travel study, and visits to RAF stations, air museums and air displays.

Apply to	the address above
Age range	From 13 yrs 9 mths to 16
Joining fee	none
Annual fee	B paid monthly
Members	about 40,000
Date started	1941

Army Cadet Force (ACF)

Cheltenham Terrace
London SW3 4RR
Tel: (01) 730 9733

In 1860, when Britain feared an invasion by the French, battalions of volunteers were formed to defend the country. In many cases boys' companies were formed as adjuncts to these battalions; it is from these that the ACF grew.

The Force is a voluntary youth organisation, sponsored by the Army, which takes part in both military and community activities. It aims to develop in its members the qualities of good citizenship and the spirit to serve both Queen and country. The ACF does this by providing adventurous and challenging activities designed to develop powers of leadership and strong character, stimulating an interest in the army, and giving encouragement and training to those thinking about a career in the regular Army, or serve in the reserve forces.

The Force is organised on a county basis with detachments of about thirty cadets, which meet in cadet huts or in schools. You can join a school detachment only if you are a pupil at that school. Cadets meet usually twice a week to parade and train, and there are occasional visits to weekend training centres. All training is based upon the Army Proficiency Certificate; this includes drill, turn-out and military knowledge, skill at arms and shooting (full bore, .22, and air rifle), use of map and compass, fieldcraft, adventurous training, first aid, and citizenship. Each county runs an annual camp of up to two weeks, and there are opportunities to travel abroad each year. Cadets also take part in local events, fund-raising and providing practical help for those in need.

As a cadet you will be able to read the *Cadet Journal and Gazette*, which comes out every two months, and includes articles, information on activities and general interest items.

Apply to the General Secretary, at the address above
Age range 13–16
Joining fee none
Annual fee none, but a small contribution to the club facilities in your detachment is expected.
Members 45,000
Date started 1930

Girls' Venture Corps (GVC)

Redhill Aerodrome
Kings Mill Lane
South Nutfield
Redhill
Surrey RH1 5JY
Tel: (0737) 823345

'Girls, do you want to develop the qualities of leadership and initiative?' If so, the Girls' Venture Corps offers you the opportunity to join one of its Units. Meetings are held once or twice a week, and you can take part in a varied programme of activities covering every aspect of the Duke of Edinburgh's Award Scheme. Unusual activities include learning about the theory of aviation, and taking part in air experience flights in small aircraft. Others include camping, canoeing, skiing, rifle-shooting, gliding, drill and dance drama.

A GVC team always takes part in the International One Hundred Mile March at Nijmegen in Holland, and there is also the chance of travelling abroad to America, Canada or Hong Kong through the International Air Cadet Exchange Scheme.

The Corps works closely with the Air Training Corps and the Army Cadet Force, taking part in joint adventure training camps. An interest in helping the local community is encouraged, too, so you may well find yourself working on a special community project.

Apply to Miss H. Prosper, Corps Director, at address above
Age range 13–16
Joining fee none
Annual fee none, you pay a small weekly subscription to your Unit
Members about 6,000
Date started 1964 when the Women's Junior Air Corps and the Girls' Training Corps merged

Sea Cadet Corps (SCC)

Broadway House
The Broadway
Wimbledon SW19 1RL
Tel: (01) 540 8222

Sea Cadets are organised on a town or city basis throughout the United Kingdom. There are 400 Units in all, each with its own name and identity just like a naval ship. Even inland Units usually have access to water and boats, and sailing and boatwork have a high priority in the Units' activities. The Corps' offshore fleet includes twenty-four sea-going vessels. There are also 2,500 inshore craft.

Units, which have both boys and girls as cadets, usually meet twice weekly and at other times for specialist training. Activities are many and include band training and contests, canoeing, canoe-building, ceremonial training, communications, cookery, electrical engineering, expeditions, first aid, general seamanship, mechanical engineering, meteorology, model-making, power boat sailing, practical seamanship, pulling boats, rifle-shooting, sea-going voyages, soccer, and swimming. All cadets can take part in adventure training, map-reading and the Duke of Edinburgh Award Scheme. Also, you can visit HM ships, go on courses held in RN training establishments, take part in sailing and pulling regattas, take part in voyages on the square-rigged sailing training vessel, the brig TS *Royalist*.

Apply to	Administrative Officer at the above address
Age range	12–16
Joining fee	none
Annual fee	none, weekly subscription of a few pence paid to Unit
Members	20,000
Date started	1899

Crusaders

Crusader House
2 Romeland Hill
St Albans
Hertfordshire AL3 4ET
Tel: (0727) 55422/3

This is a non-denominational organisation of Bible-based groups for young people, which aims to present the Christian way of life. Groups can be found all over the United Kingdom and are growing in number. There is no common place or time of meeting; groups meet in homes, halls, schools or churches, either mid-week or sometimes at weekends. The group leaders plan activities to suit their members with the aim of presenting the Christian faith in a relevant way.

There are also Crusader holidays which offer high standards of supervision, fun and action. Costs are kept to the minimum, with volunteer staff and either dormitory or tent accommodation, but the food is good and there is one member of staff to look after every three children. Activities on these holidays include surfing, games, sunbathing, tennis, badminton, treasure hunts, visits, swimming and playing music. Write and find out where your local group meets.

Apply to	Assistant Director, at the address above
Age range	9–16
Joining fee	none
Annual fee	depends on individual groups
Members	16,634
Date started	1906

Girls' Brigade (GB)

Brigade House
Parsons Green
London SW6 4TH
Tel: (01) 736 8481

This is a Christian organisation for girls. If you join, you can make new friends, learn new skills and take part in exciting new activities such as camping holidays and helping your local community. Older members can even work for the Queen's Award and the Duke of Edinburgh's Bronze, Silver and Gold Awards.

Depending on how old you are, you join either the Juniors (8-11), Seniors (11-14) or Brigaders (14+). Each of these works through a programme of spiritual, physical (for example, swimming), educational (for example, crafts and singing), and service (for example, care of pets) activities, being awarded badges to show what they have achieved.

Apply to	your local Girls' Brigade company. Ask your public library for where it meets
Age range	9–16
Joining fee	depends on the company you join
Annual fee	depends on the company you join
Members	52,168
Date started	1893

Girls' Friendly Society (GFS)

Townsend House
126 Queen's Gate
London SW7 5LQ
Tel: (01) 589 9628

Established in the nineteenth century, the aim was to provide friendship and understanding for girls who had left their village homes to work in the towns. Today this Society is bringing friendship to girls of all ages. The GFS is an Anglican organisation with branches throughout the country.

If you join a branch you can enjoy crafts, drama, expeditions, sport, and have the chance to learn about relationships, fashion and community work. You can even work for a Duke of Edinburgh's Award.

Apply to	Sandra Coleman, Director of Training, at the above address
Age range	9–16
Joining fee	further information on request
Annual fee	as above
Members	as above
Date started	1875

Methodist Association of Youth Clubs (MAYC)

2 Chester House
Pages Lane
Muswell Hill
London N10 1PR
Tel: (01) 444 9845

This is a Christian organisation which invites you to share with others in worship, study and meetings. There are over 3,500 groups, including youth clubs, choirs, prayer and Bible Study groups, drama and music groups, and youth fellowships. Your local group may be involved in helping people in your community.

When you are a member of this Association, as well as local meetings, you can join in sports, holidays and conferences, and each year in May, there is a special London weekend meeting which 12,000 members go to.

Apply to	the address above
Age range	13–16
Joining fee	none
Annual fee	none
Members	100,000
Date started	1945

Northern Ireland Association of Boys' Clubs (NIABC)

Bryson House
28 Bedford Street
Belfast
Northern Ireland BT2 7FE
Tel: (0232) 241924

If you live in Northern Ireland and want to join a boys' club, this Association will be able to tell you which of its member clubs meets near you. When you have joined a club you will be able to benefit from some of the many activities and competitions organised by the NIABC, for example, athletics, boxing, billiards, canoeing, chess, cross-country, draughts, drama, darts, fishing, football leagues, judo, quizzes, talent competitions, de facto (a new kind of competition), photography festivals, table tennis, super stars (a novelty sports day), swimming, tug of war, pool. It is also possible to enter the National Association of Boys' Clubs Fitness Award Scheme and the swimming efficiency tests operated by the NIABC.

Apply to	Mr C.E. Larmour, at the address above
Age range	10–16
Joining fee	none
Annual fee	A
Members	15,120
Date started	1940

Northern Ireland Association of Youth Clubs (NIAYC)

Hampton
Glenmachan Park
Belfast BT4 2PJ
Tel: (0232) 760067

If you live in Northern Ireland the NIAYC will be able to tell you which of its member youth clubs is near where you live, and if you then join this club you will be able to take part in many activities organised by the NIAYC. There are one day events and competitions, which include disco-dance, five-a-side football, netball, a Festival of Sport, a drama festival, fishing, and 'It's a Knockout'. Residential weekend courses are arranged, too; you could find yourself fell-walking, orienteering, walking in forests, treasure-hunting, on assault courses or night exercises, camping, bridge-building, singing or playing various games. As these weekends are planned with your club it can say what sort of weekend its members would like. The NIAYC also provides opportunities for individual groups to join in a range of international events.

Clubs receive regular information on forthcoming events and courses, and on NIAYC services, and three of four times a year *Youth News* containing news items connected to the work of clubs.

Apply to	the address above
Age range	9–16
Joining fee	none
Annual fee	small subscription paid to the clubs
Members	277 clubs, with 33,000 members
Date started	1945

Scottish Association of Youth Clubs (SAYC)

Balfour House
17 Bonnington Grove
Edinburgh EH6 4DP
Tel: (031) 554 2561

Thinking of joining a youth club in Scotland? Then write to the SAYC and ask which of their clubs meets near to where you live. Over 1,000 Scottish youth clubs belong to this Association, which aims to help young people to grow up as healthy and useful members of society through leisure time experiences. If you join a club which is a member of the SAYC you will have the chance to take part in and enjoy many leisure time activities, finding new interests and making new friends. By helping to organise and run these activities you will learn to accept and handle responsibility — good preparation for adult life.

You will receive a regular news pack keeping you up-to-date on current issues and events, and have a chance to compete in five-a-side football, netball, quizzes, darts, table tennis, badminton, volleyball, pool, uni hoc and disco dancing. There are inter-club activities through countrywide competitions and projects, plus residential weekend, one-day and evening training courses in outdoor activities, crafts and hobbies, special topics of interest, personal relationships and planning your life.

Apply to	Mr Matt Erskine, at address above
Age range	9–16
Joining fee	none
Annual fee	regular small subscriptions to clubs
Members	over 100,000
Date started	1933

Welsh Association of Youth Clubs (WAYC)

HQ and Training Centre
Sachvill Avenue
Gabalfa
Cardiff
South Glamorgan
Tel: (0222) 20396

Living in Wales and thinking about joining a youth club? Then write to the WAYC to see which of its member clubs is near to where you live. This Welsh Association has a large membership of youth clubs, including fourteen PHAB clubs for physically handicapped and able-bodied young adults, all aiming to help and educate young people in their leisure time activities. If you join a WAYC club you will be able to take part in competitions such as general knowledge quizzes, rugby 'sevens', 'super dance', 'quest' – a test of initiative and leadership, and 'postal endeavour'. Workshops are held in clubs on such interesting subjects as video filming, robotics, personal development, computer programming, parent/teenage problems, drug abuse and alcoholism, indoor games, outdoor activities, and a wide range of crafts including weaving, candle-making and pottery. In addition, there are residential training courses offering land yachting, field archery, yoga, craftwork and a commando course!

Apply to	Mr Dennis G. Frost, General Secretary at address above
Age range	9–16
Joining fee	none
Annual fee	depends on the club
Members	33,228
Date started	1935

3

Collecting

BADGES

Association of Football Badge Collectors (AFBC)

46 Ellington Drive
Gershwyn Road
Brighton Hill Rise
Basingstoke
Hampshire RG22 4EZ

Do you collect football badges? If the answer is 'yes' (or 'no, but I would like to') then this is the Association for you. The AFBA is for people who collect football club, enamel, lapel badges, and it organises conferences, meetings, and exhibitions. It is also happy to provide you with information, and if you join you will receive a monthly newsletter to keep you up-to-date with your hobby.

Apply to	the address above
Age range	further information on request
Joining fee	as above
Annual fee	as above
Members	115
Date started	1980

BADGES

Trade Union Badge Collectors' Society (TUBCS)

c/o 17 Sturdy Road
London SE15 3RH

Here is a Society which actually gives you a collection with which to start your hobby. A free selection of trade union badges, and as much advice as you want, is yours when you join. Through collecting such badges TUBCS hopes to encourage an interest in, and knowledge of, the trade union movement. If you join you will receive a newsletter produced every two months keeping you informed about your hobby; the Society also organises meetings and exhibitions for you to go along to.

Apply to	the address above
Age range	9–16
Joining fee	none
Annual fee	free
Members	30
Date started	1980

British Beermat Collectors' Society (BBCS)

68 Fenton Close
Waldridge Park
Chester-le-Street
County Durham DH2 3JD
Tel: (0385) 885592

You may not be old enough to drink beer, but you can still collect beermats and other drip mats! Tegestology is the odd name given to this hobby, although collectors have also been dubbed 'dripsomaniacs'. The largest collection in the world is said to contain more than 72,000 mats, so there is plenty of scope for collecting!

The highlight of the year is an annual international meeting where over a million beermats are included in one gigantic swapping session; as a member you will be able to take part in this. You will also receive *Beermat Magazine* each month, with details of local area meetings throughout the country, articles and news of new mats. There is also an opportunity to advertise your wants and swaps.

Apply to	Mr D. Walton, at the address above
Age range	9–16
Joining fee	A
Annual fee	C
Members	1,200
Date started	1960

Old Bottle Club of Great Britain (OBC of GB)

2 Strafford Avenue
Elsegar
Barnsley
South Yorkshire S74 8AA
Tel: (0226) 745156

Old bottles, pots, and pot lids are very much part of British history; for instance they tell us what people used to eat and drink, and how food and drink was stored. The OBC encourages the recovery and study of old bottles and containers.

If you join you will receive a glossy magazine, *British Bottle Review*, four times a year; it includes news of latest finds, shows, and the many regional clubs throughout the United Kingdom. Exhibitions of collections are held throughout the country, with a large National Weekend Exhibition every two years. The Club also produces books on the subject to help you with your collecting.

Apply to	Mr A.R. Blakeman, at the address above
Age range	9–16
Joining fee	none
Annual fee	B
Members	2,000
Date started	about 1975

Cartophilic Society of Great Britain Ltd.

The Pines
Springfield Road
Camberley
Surrey GU15 1AB

Interested in collecting cigarette and trade cards? This Society, with over thirty branches and clubs throughout Great Britain, is devoted to encouraging the hobby of collecting cards issued with cigarettes and other products. If you join this Society the magazine *Cartophil Notes and News* will be sent to you six times a year, and you can take part in meetings, and use the Society's library.

Apply to	Mr Derek Jenkins, at the address above
Age range	9–16
Joining fee	none
Annual fee	B
Members	830
Date started	1938

Cigarette Packet Collectors' Club of Great Britain

15 Dullingham Road
Newmarket
Suffolk CB8 9JT
Tel: (01) 940 2404 (daytime)
(01) 759 2797 (evenings)

Smoking is not at all good for you, but collecting cigarette packets can be fun. The aims of this Club are to help collectors to obtain packets, to advise on how best to keep and display them, and to give information about the age, rarity of packets and about the tobacco industry generally.

Although collectors are adults, many of them in fact began in the 1950s; there was something of a schoolboy craze for collecting cigarette packets with the fronts forming a substitute for cigarette cards which had been discontinued due to the war. However the future of the hobby does seem certain with an encouraging number of young people showing an interest today.

If you join you will receive a magazine, *The Cigarette Packet*, four times a year. It contains a wealth of illustrations along with interesting articles and members advertisements for buying, selling or exchanging items. A copy of the membership list is sent to all who join the Club, providing brief details of age, particular interests, and types of packet collected, so you can find out which members share your interests. Opportunities to buy packets — at prices starting as low as 10p — are provided at Club meetings, which are advertised in the magazine.

No one knows how many different cigarette packets there are. Several collections number over 50,000 items. One such collection was made by a Danish lawyer named Niels Ventegodt and it is listed in the *Guinness Book of Records* as containing the world's oldest and rarest packets. However, even a small collection will almost certainly contain something that even the keenest collector does not have. Practice in arranging a collection (and being able to read foreign names on the

packets) are all skills that can be furthered by collecting packets. The pleasure you get from your collection will not just depend on how many you have but on the amount of care and enthusiasm you put into it.

Apply to	Mr Hilary Humphries, at the address above
Age range	9–16
Joining fee	none
Annual fee	B
Members	107
Date started	1980

British Numismatic Society (BNS)

63 West Way
Edgware
Middlesex HA8 9LA
Tel: (01) 958 8752

The BNS is for you if you are interested in coins struck or used in Great Britain and Ireland, from the introduction of coinage into Britain in the first century BC down to modern times. It's also for you if you are interested in medals and tokens, or in coins of the present and former British overseas territories and dependencies. If you join BNS you will receive the annual *British Numismatic Journal*, which provides results of the most recent research into the history of coins and describes new discoveries. If you live near London there are regular meetings to go to from September to June, at which papers are read and exhibitions held. There is also a big library of books on coins which you can consult.

Apply to	Mr W. Slater, Honorary Secretary, at the address above
Age range	older readers
Joining fee	none
Annual fee	C
Members	529
Date started	1903

Commemorative Collectors' Society (CSS)

25 Farndale Close
Long Eaton
Near Nottingham NG10 3PA
Tel: (0602) 727666

Events and important occasions have been recorded by man since early history and 'popular commemoratives' are one way of doing this. A popular commemorative is an item which has been made for sale to the public, marking or commemorating any event, occasion or person of the times, anywhere in the world. It may be a mug, plate, thimble, book, tankard — in fact almost anything. Royal events such as weddings, have always been a popular subject for such souvenirs. Popular commemorative items tell us about the times in which they were produced.

If you join the CSS you will receive a newsletter four to six times a year, and *Collecting Memorabilia*, a quarterly magazine. This contains articles by experts, details and background information on new items to be issued, and news of all matters concerned with collecting antique and modern souvenirs anywhere in the world. Also you will be able to hear speakers at regular meetings, and attend special exhibitions. On great occasions, such as a Royal wedding, when a large number of souvenirs is to be issued, the Society publishes a special review, listing the various items to be issued to help you to add to your collection.

Apply to	Mr S.N.Jackson, Secretary, at the address above
Age range	9–16
Joining fee	none
Annual fee	C
Members	6,751
Date started	1972

Labologists' Society

211 Pinewood Park
Cove
Farnborough
Hampshire GU14 9LQ
Tel: (0252) 40935

Members of this Society collect labels from beer, wine, spirit, mineral water and soft drink bottles, and from cheese. They may also collect matchbox and hotel labels. Some even collect trays, posters, bottles, photographs, badges, beer pump clips, key rings, bottle openers, jugs and beer mats — all connected with breweries. Many members are interested in the history of brewing.

If you join this Society, you can go to meetings held in London or maybe near where you live. At these meetings, you can swap items from your collection, and talk about collecting. Every two months, you will be sent a newsletter which has features on old breweries and labels, and includes information about new labels.

Apply to	Mr R. Denison, 24 Pennypiece, Goring-on-Thames Reading, Oxfordshire
Age range	9–16
Joining fee	B
Annual fee	B
Members	about 300
Date started	1958

British Matchbox, Label, and Booklet Society (BMLBS)

22 Githa Road
Hastings
East Sussex TN35 5JU
Tel: (0424) 431236

This Society provides matchbox collectors with a newsletter every two months, exhibitions and meetings in many parts of Britain, including London, and a library and bookshop. There is a special junior section, so write now and find out more about this interesting hobby.

Apply to	the address above
Age range	9–16
Joining fee	none
Annual fee	B
Members	about 900
Date started	1945

The British Philatelic Federation Limited (BPF)

314 Vauxhall Bridge Road
London SW1V 1AA
Tel: (01) 828 4416

When you join the BBF you will receive every two months the magazine *Stamp News*, and each year the year-book, a directory of societies, and a handbook. You also get free or reduced admission to national exhibitions, and a chance to attend the Congress held every year in a different provincial centre, bringing together 'stamping' with social activities.

If you collect stamps on a particular theme or themes you can also join the British Thematic Association (BTA) free of charge, and receive their publication *Themescene*.

Apply to	the address above
Age range	9–16
Joining fee	none
Annual fee	C
Members	about 1,000
Date started	1976

British Postmark Society (BPS)

9 Gainsborough Avenue
Marple Bridge
Stockport
Cheshire SK6 5BW
Tel: (061) 4271890

If you collect British postal markings, particularly those of the present century, then the BPS is for you. The types of postmark

which can be collected include slogans, special event marks, machine marks, forces mail, handstamps, paid machine marks, and mobile post office marks. A regular illustrated *Bulletin* will be sent to you four times a year, full of articles, lists and news. Further information is available to you through regular meetings in London, the use of a good library, and occasional publications. Each year there is a special postal auction, and a mini-auction follows the Annual General Meeting. The Society also holds an Annual Cup Competition which you can enter with some of your collection.

Apply to	Mr A.J. Howard Honorary Secretary, at the address above
Age range	9–16
Joining fee	A
Annual fee	B
Members	320
Date started	1958

The Letter-Box Study Group (LBSG)

c/o 43 Miall Road
Hall Green
Birmingham B28 9BS
Tel: (021) 777 7062
(after 6 pm or weekends)

Collecting information about letter-boxes may seem an unusual hobby, but it can be most interesting, and needs a good deal of detective work. This Group aims to gather and make available information on all aspects of letter-boxes. With the help of its members it carries out surveys of rare and historical boxes, and these have resulted in some notable finds of boxes not known to have existed before. So far the group's 'listing' includes 330 different models.

If you join the LBSG you will receive a newsletter giving details of the latest information collected by members, photographs available, details of members, and sometimes a postcard showing an unusual box. The Group also tries to obtain supplies of postcards, new and used, showing letter-boxes issued by the Post Office, and tries to let you know of stamps showing letter-boxes and of any commercially produced items made as replicas of boxes.

Apply to	Mrs S.J. Jones, Secretary at the address above
Age range	9–16
Joining fee	none
Annual fee	B
Members	about 400
Date started	1976

The Postcard Club of Great Britain

34 Harper House
St James Crescent
London SW9 7LW
Tel: (01) 733 0720

This Club encourages the collecting of postcards as a hobby, and as a means of making friends all over the world. If you join you will be able to go to meetings and exhibitions, and every two months you will receive *Postcard World*, a magazine to help you with your hobby.

Apply to	Mrs Drene Brennan, at the address above
Age range	9–16
Joining fee	none
Annual fee	B
Members	750
Date started	1961

United Kingdom Spoon Collectors Club (UKSCC)

72 Edinburgh Road
Newmarket
Suffolk CB8 0QD
Tel: (0636) 665457

The word 'spoon' originally meant a chip of wood or horn carved from a larger piece. The Greeks and Romans used permanent materials, such as bronze and silver, to make their spoons, and there is evidence that ancient Egyptians used art and cosmetic spoons. Throughout history the spoon has been designed to be not only functional but decorative. Today you can collect a wide range of souvenir spoons, designed to be collected rather than used.

This Club provides an opportunity for spoon collectors to contact one another informally and at a conference. As a member, every two months, you will receive *Spoonerama*, a magazine full of useful information to help you with your collecting.

Apply to	Mr David Cross, at the address above
Age range	9–16
Joining fee	further information available on request
Annual fee	as above
Members	460
Date started	1980

Thimble Society of London

c/o Grays Antiques
58 Davies Street
London W1
Tel: (01) 493 0560

Thimbles, tape measures, lace bobbins, pin cushions, clamps, chatelaines, needlecases, shuttles and sewing boxes are the sort of things which members of this Society collect. Members receive a magazine four times a year. From this, by mail order, thimbles and other sewing items — dating from the thirteenth century to the present day and ranging in price from 50p to £500 — can be bought.

Also included in the magazine are articles on restoring, cataloguing, investment, security and how to date sewing items, as well as a letters page. Talks are given to members at coffee mornings, and once a year you can attend a lecture with slides. An added attraction is that the Society issues its own limited edition of Collectors' Thimbles and silver souvenirs of special events such as the recent birth of Prince Henry, which you can buy and add to your collection.

Apply to	the Secretary at the address above
Age range	9–16
Joining fee	none
Annual fee	B
Members	700
Date started	1981

4

Crafts

HANDWRITING

Society for Italic Handwriting (SIH)

4/75 Torrington Park
London N12 9PN

Italic handwriting is a simple, modern and elegant way to write. It is simple enough to be taught to young children, and modern enough to be used today. This Society encourages italic handwriting by holding meetings, arranging handwriting competitions, courses of instruction and mounting exhibitions.

If you join the SIH, you will receive an annual magazine, as well as a regular newsletter.

Apply to	the Membership Dept, SIH, c/o Berol Ltd, Oldmedow Road, King's Lynn, PE30 4JR
Age range	9–16
Joining fee	C
Annual fee	B
Members	about 900
Date started	1954

KITES

The Kite Society (BKS)

31 Grange Road
Ilford
Essex IG1 1EU
Tel: (01) 478 6668

Interested in kites? If so, then the BKS has a lot to offer. When you join you will receive a quarterly newsletter *The Kite Flier*, which includes letters, news and details of local and national events to be held around the country. There are trips organised to international

kite festivals which you can take part in, too. You also get public liability insurance cover, and special discounts at kite shops throughout the United Kingdom and Europe.

Apply to	the address above
Age range	9–16
Joining fee	none
Annual fee	B
Members	650
Date started	1979

Marquetry Society

The Barn House
Llanon
Nr Aberystwyth
Dyfed SY23 5LZ
Tel: (09748) 581

Marquetry is the craft and art of making pictures, designs and patterns by the skilful use of the grain, figure and natural colours of the veneers of wood. The separate parts of the picture or design are cut to shape, assembled and glued to a prepared base or background. Marquetry was developed as a pictorial hobby about fifty years ago. Now, this craft is used to make not only pictures, but trays, coffee tables, and jewellery boxes.

The Marquetry Society has a growing membership and has formed groups throughout the country where members meet to swop ideas and to learn from one another. Members receive a quarterly magazine, *Marquetarian*, which contains articles, line drawings, and letters. You also have free entry to the national exhibition held each year at a different place, and the right to exhibit your own work if you wish. The Society also offers free advice by a panel of experts on every subject related to marquetry.

Apply to	the Secretary at the address above
Age range	11–16
Joining fee	A
Annual fee	C
Members	about 1,000
Date started	1952

British Origami Society (BOS)

12 Thorn Road
Bramhall
Stockport SK7 1HQ
Tel: (061) 439 2486

Origami is a Japanese word; *ori* means to fold, and *gami* means paper. The art of origami, or paper-folding, in fact started in Japan; it is possible to make all sorts of things such as animals, insects, boxes, decorations and flowers, through this skilful craft. According to BOS origami is an art limited only by the imagination and ingenuity of the folder.

BOS holds exhibitions and workshops, where you can fold models as well as see them folded. When you join BOS you can help with these, including for international exhibitions. You also can enjoy a two to three day convention where you can meet other members, do a great deal of folding, swop ideas and talk about your art. Many places also have 'mini-meetings' held in members' homes, and special meetings to welcome and 'fold' with distinguished visitors from overseas.

You may borrow from the BOS library, which has been built up over the last fifteen years, and includes books, magazines and unpublished instructions. You can also buy (at special low prices) paper, books and other items not available anywhere else in the United Kingdom including unusual foreign books and excellent Japanese paper. Last, but by no means least, you receive six times a year the magazine *British Origami*, filled with articles, news, letters and models, diagrams and illustations.

Apply to	Dave Brill, Honorary Secretary at the address above
Age range	9–16
Joining fee	none
Annual fee	C
Members	400
Date started	1967

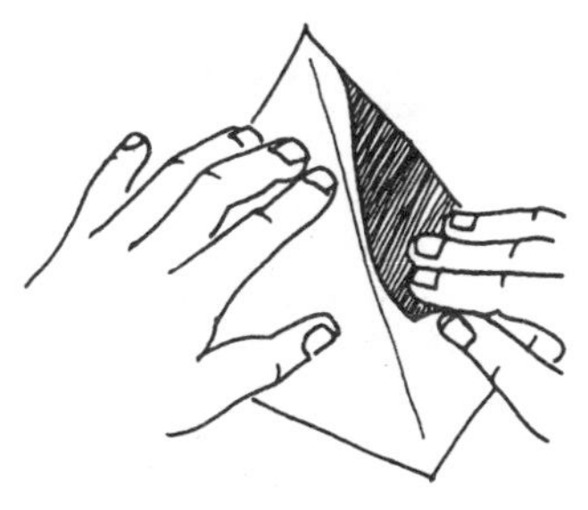

British Puppet and Model Theatre Guild (BPMTG)

18 Maple Road
Yeading
Nr Hayes
Middlesex UB4 9LP

This Guild promotes the use of puppets and model theatres, raises the standards of puppetry, and makes it possible for its members, both amateur and professional puppeteers, to meet and swap ideas. When you join the BPMTG you can attend meetings and take part in weekend schools, as well as exhibitions and festivals held throughout Britain. You can also use the large library containing all kinds of books about puppetry and the puppet theatre. Once a month you will receive a newsletter and the Guild's *The Puppet Master*, as well as a Puppet Technical Sheet, all sent free!

Apply to	Mr Gordon Shapley, Honorary Secretary at the address above
Age range	9–16
Joining fee	none
Annual fee	B
Members	315
Date started	1925

Wood Carvers' Association (WCA)

15 Princes Road
Ealing
London W13 9AS

If you enjoy woodcarving you may like to join this association, which encourages woodcarving and wood sculpture. Members receive the *Wood Carvers' Newsletter* six times a year, and can call upon the association for information and advice.

Apply to	the address above
Age range	older readers
Joining fee	further information on request
Annual fee	as above
Members	600
Date started	1971

Use this letter as a guide if you want to write to a national organisation about joining. Address your letter to The Secretary, and don't forget to include your own name and address.

Dear Sir (or Madam)

My hobby is   and I want to belong to a society that can help me learn more about it. Could you please send me details of how I can join the *(put in the name of the organisation)*? I enclose a stamped addressed envelope for your reply. Thank you.

I found your address in *Where to Join*.

Yours faithfully

5

Fitness & Health

FIRST AID

British Red Cross Society (BRCS)

9 Grosvenor Crescent
London SW1X 7EJ
Tel: (01) 235 5454

Accidents in the home or on the road — would you know how to help? As a junior or youth member of the Red Cross you will learn about accident prevention, first aid and nursing. Also you can decide to learn about infant and child care, health and hygiene, drill and rescue, fire protection, home mechanics and camping.

The Red Cross provides opportunities for you to help in hospitals and old people's homes, visit handicapped children and take them on specially organised holidays, and to be involved with projects to help overseas branches and developing Red Cross societies.

This is a worldwide movement with a common aim, 'to prevent and relieve suffering, regardless of nationality, race or religious beliefs'. If you are aged five to ten years you can join a Red Cross Junior Group, and ten to eighteen years old, the Red Cross Youth Group. As a member you can wear a uniform and take part in activities and various training courses, and receive *Red Cross News*. Write now and find out where your nearest group meets.

Apply to	the address above
Age range	9–16
Joining fee	none
Annual fee	none
Members	110,345
Date started	1890

Casualties Union (CU)

1 Grosvenor Crescent
London SW1X 7EE
Tel: (01) 235 5366

The aim of the Casualties Union is 'that wherever first aid is taught there shall be a group of trained casualties to assist'. These casualties bring a touch of realism to training.

If you want to join the CU you must hold at least one certificate in first aid, and be prepared to learn more about the body and first aid treatments.

The Union is organised into branches and study circles, and as a member of these you receive training in how to be a realistic 'casualty'. To start with you are a probationer until you take your first proficiency test and then you may be offered full membership. Once fully trained you could find yourself acting as a casualty for the fire brigade, first aid competitions, farm safety exhibitions, rail crash exercises, or even in films!

All members receive the magazine *Casualty Simulation* quarterly.

Apply to	the Hon. Secretary, at the address above
Age range	9–16
Joining fee	none
Annual fee	B
Members	2,000
Date started	1942

Casualties Union

St Andrew's Ambulance Association (St AAA)

48 Milton Street
Glasgow G4 0HR
Tel: (041) 332 4031

As the leading voluntary first aid movement operating within Scotland, this organisation runs, at many locations, a junior section known as St Andrew's Ambulance Association Cadet Corps. When

you join you will learn the elementary principles of First Aid, Home Nursing and Hygiene, leading to Junior First Aid and Home Nursing certificates, and may be able to enter the Association's competitions.

Apply to	Mr J.W.R. Cunningham, at the address above
Age range	9–16
Joining fee	none
Annual fee	none for 9–15
Members	4,150
Date started	1882

St John Ambulance Association and Brigade

1 Grosvenor Crescent
London SW1X 7EF
Tel: (01) 235 5231

You may have seen members of this Association when you have visited county shows, the theatre, football matches, or other public events. They are on hand if anyone becomes ill or injured. Maybe you have wondered about training in first aid so that you too could help?

St John's provides such training, and organises competitions you can enter. Write now for more information; the Association will be pleased to help, and to tell you where your nearest branch meets.

Apply to	the address above
Age range	9–16
Joining fee	none
Annual fee	none
Members	62,000
Date started	1887

National Jogging Association (NJA)

Westlake Cottage
Newstead Abbey Park
Nottinghamshire NG15 8GE
Tel: (0623) 793496

Jogging requires no special equipment, skill or ability. You can do it anywhere and at any time.

The Jogging Award Scheme, introduced in September 1979 and sponsored by Adidas, is the way that the NJA encourages people of all ages to take up jogging. You can work for these awards on your own or with your school. All you have to do is keep a record of the time you spend jogging, and as this time grows you earn different badges, until reaching Super Jogger, a gold badge which you get for 250 hours of jogging. Write now to the NJA and find out how to start collecting your badges — and get fit at the same time!

Apply to	the address above
Age range	9–16
Joining fee	none
Annual fee	none
Date started	1978

Medau Society

86 Robson House
East Street
Epsom
Surrey KT17 1HH
Tel: (03727) 29056

Medau rhythmic movement began in Germany, and is exercise which gives you a feeling of well-being, relaxation and enjoyment. Medau classes are held in many parts of Britain, especially as part of adult education classes, although some schools have teachers who have been trained to give classes.

When you join this Society, you can go to rallies, weekend and holiday courses, workshops lecture-demonstrations. If you want to keep fit and enjoy a graceful activity, write to the Medau Society and see if classes are held in your area.

Apply to the address above
Age range 9–16
Joining fee varies depending on where you join
Annual fee D
Members about 9,000
Date started 1952

Vegetarian Society of the United Kingdom (VSUK)

53 Marloes Road
Kensington
London W8 6LA
Tel: (01) 937 7739

Vegetarianism is not so much a hobby, more a way of life. However, if you are a vegetarian or are thinking about becoming one, joining this Society can help you. When you join you will receive a magazine, *Vegetarian*, which is full of recipes, news, good ideas, articles, and information about meetings and courses. The Society organises cookery courses, residential weekends and dozens of other activities through its branches all over Britain. There is also a free *International Vegetarian Handbook* which is sent to you, and this provides you with information on hotels and restaurants both in the United Kingdom, and abroad.

Apply to the address above
Age range 12–16
Joining fee none
Annual fee B
Members 10,500
Date started 1969

British Amateur Weightlifters Association (BAWLA)

3 Iffley Turn
Oxford OX4 4DU
Tel: (0865) 778319

BAWLA brings together all amateur weightlifters. Amongst the services it offers is a Schools Badge Scheme in Weightlifting, designed for those starting weight-training and eventually moving on to weightlifting. You must be over thirteen years old to take part in this scheme, which gives you the chance to earn bronze, silver and gold badges as your skills develop.

When beginning weightlifting you should join a club which belongs to BAWLA, so that you get the right sort of training, learn the rules about competitions, and keep a record of attendances, training schedules, work accomplished, details of coaching, and attendances at events and courses.

Interested? Then write to BAWLA and find out where your nearest club meets.

Apply to	the address above
Age range	older readers
Joining fee	none
Annual fee	B
Members	12,000
Date started	1910

British Wheel of Yoga (BWOY)

1 Hamilton Place
Boston Road
Sleaford
Lincs NG34 7ES
Tel: (0529) 306851

When you join the British Wheel of Yoga you receive the quarterly magazine *Spectrum* full of interesting articles and information, a regular newsletter telling you 'what's on', personal insurance cover, a free sew-on Wheel badge, and regular notices of all Wheel activities. Also you can obtain free advice about yoga, and be admitted at special low prices to national and international events.

Apply to	Mrs J.M. Scales, Honorary General Secretary 15 Station Avenue Warwick, CV34 5HJ
Age range	older readers
Joining fee	further information on request
Annual fee	as above
Members	about 4,000
Date started	1973

NOTES

6

Pets

BUDGERIGARS

The Budgerigar Society

49/53 Hazelwood Road
Northampton NN1 1LG
Tel: (0604) 24549

The budgerigar originally came from the warm regions of the world, particularly from Australia. These very colourful, clean, easily and cheaply looked-after birds make excellent pets. If you want to know more about budgerigars, or wish to breed or show them, then this is the Society for you.

As a member you will receive *The Budgerigar* six times a year, full of interesting articles, reports, photographs, news and letters. The Society also offers advice, registers breeders, issues coded rings, helps with research, and supports shows by providing prizes, rosettes and certificates. Many people keep budgerigars, and here is a chance for you to ensure that this delightful pet is also an interesting hobby.

Apply to	Mr Alan Crook, General Secretary, at the address above
Age range	10–16
Joining fee	B
Annual fee	B
Members	6,200
Date started	1925

CATS

The Cats Protection League

17 Kings Road
Horsham
West Sussex RH13 5PP
Tel: (0403) 65566

It is known that cats lived in the wild as far back as seven million years ago, and that domestic cats date back several thousand years to ancient Egypt. The earliest record of domestic cats in Great Britain is dated AD 936, when Howel Dda, Prince of South Central Wales, introduced laws for their protection.

It is never too early to start caring for cats, and members of the Cats Protection League are helping in the rescue of stray, unwanted and injured cats and finding them new homes. The League has seven cat shelters in Surrey, Essex, Kent, Sussex,

Derbyshire, Devon and the Isle of Wight. These provide purpose-built accommodation, some catering for elderly and other cats for which homes cannot be found. All the shelters have kitten houses, isolation units and treatment areas. The League is also very active in telling the public about the care of cats and kittens, and produces a variety of helpful free leaflets and pamphlets.

If you join the League, every two months you will receive the magazine *The Cat*, which includes articles, poems, stories, competitions, photographs, letters and news from the League's headquarters and its 140 branches and groups.

Apply to	Mrs T. Strange, at the address above
Age range	9–16
Joining fee	none
Annual fee	B
Members	14,000
Date started	1927

Feline Advisory Bureau (FAB)
350 Upper Richmond Road
Putney
London SW15 6TL
Tel: (01) 789 9553

Caring about cats is what FAB is all about. The Bureau has two aims – to advise cat owners on how to keep their cats healthy and happy and to provide special funding to investigate cat diseases. It helps to pay for a veterinary surgeon to specialise in cat medicine at the University of Bristol Veterinary School.

If you join FAB you will receive a *Bulletin* four times a year; this contains scientific papers and general interest articles. FAB also publishes many special leaflets and booklets on cat care and cat disease, and organises conferences and regional meetings which you can go along to and hear specialists speaking on cats. You can also obtain a list of approved boarding catteries.

By joining this Bureau you not only find out about how to look after your cat, but know that you are helping the understanding of cat illness and to improve its treatment.

Apply to	Mrs Betty Thomas, General Secretary, at address above
Age range	9–16
Joining fee	none
Annual fee	D
Members	2,000
Date started	1958

United Kingdom Feline Register UK Cat Club (UKFR)

87 Mandale Road
Kinson
Bournemouth
Dorset BH11 8HZ
Tel: (0202) 529777

If you are thinking of buying a cat, the Feline Register can provide you with helpful information on cat breeds and breeders, and what to look for when buying your kitten. It registers pedigree cats and kittens, and provides advice to those wishing to breed cats at home. To help you, useful leaflets are produced on common cat illnesses, your first kitten, and your cat having kittens.

Apply to	Mr W. Brandwood, at the address above
Age range	9–16
Joining fee	none
Annual fee	free
Members	about 600
Date started	1981

Kennel Club Junior Organisation (KCJO)

1–5 Clarges Street
Piccadilly
London W1Y 8AB
Tel: (01) 493 6651

You do not have to own a dog to join this Club, you just need to be interested in dogs and their care and training. If you join the KCJO you will be able to go on visits (organised regionally) to shows, trials, dog-training centres, local kennels, dog sanctuaries, and to other dog activities. You will be able to learn about the care and training of dogs from experts, such as veterinary surgeons and dog-training instructors. If you own a dog you can take part in agility and obedience competitions. Each year a quiz competition is held, the winning teams from each region competing to become national KCJO Champions.

The KCJO also runs an Award Scheme. In order to compete you have to keep a log-book recording your achievements in feeding and general care, handling experience at competitions, trials or in the show ring, experience of training and stewarding, training classes and meetings attended, judging experience, and taking part in or attending any other dog events. You also have to complete a personal project on dogs. A satisfactory log-book receives a Regional Certificate, and the best three books from each region each year will be judged for the gold, silver and bronze awards. The gold awards are presented at Cruft's Dog Show.

Apply to	the Membership Secretary at the above address, or if you live in Scotland to Mr J.A. Johnston, 76 Kilnford Drive, Dundonald, Ayrshire
Age range	9–16
Joining fee	none
Annual fee	B
Members	1,165
Date started	1985

National Canine Defence League (NCDL)

1 Pratt Mews
London NW1 0AD
Tel: (01) 388 0137

When joining the NCDL you help it to campaign for the welfare of dogs and provide homes for lost, abandoned and neglected dogs.

As a dog owner you can benefit in other ways, too. You will get free public liability insurance up to £1,500,000 against damage or injury which may be caused by your dog, a free identification disc with your address and dog's name if you wish, the NCDL veterinary guarantee in case of accident, and free advice and general information on how best to look after your dog. If you wish, your dog can be buried in one of the League's cemeteries. Also, every two months, you will receive a newsletter, full of interesting articles and news about the League's work, and letters from members.

Apply to	Miss J. Harris, at the above address
Age range	9–16
Joining fee	none
Annual fee	B
Members	14,000
Date started	1891

National Dog Owners' Association

39–41 North Road
Islington
London N7 9DB
Tel: (01) 609 2757

This is a long-established voluntary organisation which has much to offer today's dog owner. As a member you are offered veterinary fees insurance (which covers your vet bills if your pet becomes sick), and you get automatic insurance cover if your dog is involved in causing an accident. You receive a magazine *Dog News and Family Pets*, six times a year, newsletters, advice, and invitations to annual open days and exemption dog shows.

Information is available on selecting and caring for your dog, training and exhibiting. As a member of this Association you receive many benefits, but you also support its work in trying to find homes for stray and unwanted dogs with caring people.

Apply to	Mr Doug Palmer-Moore at the address above, including a stamped self-addressed envelope
Age range	9–16
Joining fee	none
Annual fee	C
Members	12,500
Date started	1953

British Marine Aquarist Association (BMAA)

139 Bradford Avenue
Greatfield Estate
Hull HU9 4LZ
Tel: (0482) 799980

The BMAA is specially for those of you who are interested in keeping marine fish and fauna in your aquariums. It organises exhibitions, competitions, meetings and visits which you could take part in; write and ask for further information.

Apply to	the address above
Age range	older readers
Joining fee	none
Annual fee	C
Members	515
Date started	1970

Federation of British Aquatic Societies (FBAS)

2 Cedar Avenue
Wickford
Essex SS12 9DT

Are you interested in keeping, breeding and showing fish? If yes, then FBAS will be able to put you in contact with your local club.

Apply to	the address above
Age range	older readers
Joining fee	paid by clubs
Annual fee	paid by clubs
Members	190 clubs
Date started	1938

The Parrot Society

19A De Parys Avenue
Bedford
Bedfordshire MK40 2TX
Tel: (0234) 58922

This Society has as its aims the study and conservation of all parrots and parrot-like birds, other than the domestic budgerigar. It is keen to help the beginner, and has published three booklets on Australian parrakeets, cockatoos and parrots, and African greys, to help anyone keeping these birds. There is also a monthly magazine, which contains interesting articles and letters describing the experiences of members, and is of interest to the expert and beginner alike. The magazine also includes wants, sales and swaps of parrots and scarce birds the dealers do not handle, and as a member you can advertise free of charge.

There are about fifteen area groups which meet to discuss problems, attend film shows and lectures, and go on visits. The Parrot Society can tell you where your nearest group meets.

Apply to	the Secretary, at the address above
Age range	9–16
Joining fee	none
Annual fee	C
Members	4,500
Date started	1966

The Parrot Society

National Pigeon Association (NPA)

12 Birdsholt Close
Skellingthorpe
Lincoln LN6 5XF
Tel: (0522) 689246

The NPA caters for more than 600 varieties of fancy and flying pigeons, many of which are old breeds from the United Kingdom. Its aim is to breed and exhibit birds at shows throughout the country. It makes rules about the issue of rings, the organisation of shows (particularly championship shows), and the exhibiting of pigeons. Challenge certificates are issued to championship shows: if a bird wins three of these the owner can have it recognised as a champion. The NPA also issues a magazine to its members called *Feathered World*, which contains articles, advertisements, breed clubs and a breeders' register. This is a hobby you can enjoy all year through. If you are thinking of taking it up the NPA will send you a helpful booklet about keeping and breeding pigeons, and put you in touch with breed clubs and local societies.

Apply to	Mr E.H. Whitehead, Carnia, 85 Fairways, West Shore, Llandudno, Gwynedd, North Wales LL30 2HX Tel: (0492) 74723
Age range	9–16
Joining fee	none
Annual fee	B
Members	800
Date started	1918

Royal Pigeon Racing Association (RPRA)

The Reddings
Nr Cheltenham
Gloucestershire GL51 6RN
Tel: (0452) 713529

If you are interested in long distance pigeon-racing, this is the Association for you. When you join the RPRA you receive each week *The British Homing World*, 'Britain's premier pigeon weekly'. This is full of news, letters, articles, reports from clubs and information about forthcoming races. If you want to join a local club the RPRA can tell you where your nearest club meets. Many pigeon clubs welcome young members and can help with advice about equipment and pigeons.

Apply to	Major E.C. Camilleri (Ret'd), General Manager, at the address above
Age range	9–16
Joining fee	none
Annual fee	A
Members	67,666
Date started	1896

National Fancy Rat Society (NFRS)

18 Browns Lane
Uckfield
East Sussex TN22 1RY
Tel: (0825) 4537

Rats are the most intelligent, gentle and affectionate pets, as anyone who has kept them will tell you. They seldom, if ever, bite. Today's 'fancy rats' are descended from the wild brown rat, which arrived in Britain around 1714. Queen Victoria's Royal Rat Catcher, Jack Black, was the first man to breed what may be called fancy rats. The first exhibiting of fancy rats came about when a Miss Mary Douglas, in early 1900, suggested including classes for fancy rats within the Mouse Club. So in 1901 the first classes for fancy rats were staged at Aylesbury, Buckinghamshire, and Miss Douglas had her reward when her fancy rat won Best Rat in the show. Now, this Society alone holds about twenty shows a year.

The Society welcomes breeders and pet-keepers as members. When you join you receive a bi-monthly magazine *Pro-Rat-A*. Each month shows are organised where you can exhibit your rats. If you want to buy rats, the Society has a list of members who breed them, and advertisements for rats can be found in the magazine. However, the best way is to visit a show and choose a pair, having seen the many types that are available. If you have any problems with your rats you can get advice from the NFRS, whether you telephone or write.

Apply to	Mrs Jenny Cléroux at the address above
Age range	9–16
Joining fee	none
Annual fee	B
Members	328
Date started	1976

British Tarantula Society

36 Phillimore Place
Radlett
Hertfordshire WD7 8NL
Tel: (0923) 48995 days, (09276) 6071 evenings and weekends

You either like spiders, or you do not! If you do, and even if you are not lucky enough to own a tarantula, you could join this society.

A tarantula needs remarkably little care. It only needs about one feed a week in addition to fresh water always on hand. There are no messy problems and it does not have to be taken for a walk! It carries no diseases communicable to man or domestic livestock. It is a noiseless creature and actually most species are quite docile. If it does bite (which is very rare) its bite is like a wasp sting, and so only those unfortunate enough to be allergic to such stings should keep away.

When you join this Society you receive a newsletter every two months full of useful information. Each year a meeting is held when talks and discussions take place.

Apply to	Mrs Ann Webb, Secretary, at the address above
Age range	9–16
Joining fee	none
Annual fee	C
Members	over 100
Date started	1984

NOTES

7

Natural History

The Irish Society for the Prevention of Cruelty to Animals (ISPCA)

1 Grand Canal Quay
Dublin 2
Tel: (0001) 775922

ISPCA aims to prevent and lessen the suffering of pets and wild animals. It brings together the work of thirty societies in Ireland, all advising on, and helping with, problems relating to animals. These societies also collect, shelter and find new homes for stray and unwanted cats and dogs, and provide treatments for sick and injured animals and birds. ISPCA also provides shelter for sick and/or disabled horses, ponies and donkeys at a 24-acre farm at Liscarrol, County Cork.

By joining this Society — and you do not have to live in Ireland to do so — you can help it in its work. You will receive leaflets about caring for pets which you can also pass on to your friends. You can help with fund-raising, such as flag days, sales of work, and having a collection box in your home.

Apply to	the Administrator, at the address above
Age range	9–16
Joining fee	none
Annual fee	B
Members	further information on request

Royal Society for the Prevention of Cruelty to Animals (RSPCA)

Causeway
Horsham
West Sussex RH12 1HG
Tel: (0403) 64181

On the evening of 16th June 1824, this Society was begun to prevent cruelty and promote kindness to animals. If you love and care for *all* animals, and would like to be involved in their welfare, you will enjoy being a member of the Junior RSPCA.

As a member you will receive, six times a year, the magazine *Animal World*. It includes interesting articles on animal life and care, a letters page, news of other members' fund raising, book reviews, quizzes, and a penfriend column. The RSPCA also publishes booklets and posters on caring for animals, which you can buy.

When you join the RSPCA you are sent a special membership badge, certificate and passbook.

Inside the passbook there is space for you to put your Care Award stickers, which you get by answering ten questions correctly in each issue of *Animal World*. When you have earned seven stickers you are sent a special badge and certificate. And you will have learned a lot about looking after animals!

As a member of the RSPCA you will know that your subscription is helping to work against animal cruelty, to provide advice on animal care, and to find homes for unwanted animals.

Apply to	Miss Cindy Milburn, at the address above
Age range	9–16
Joining fee	none
Annual fee	B
Members	25,000
Date started	1824

Wildlife Sound Recording Society

c/o British Library of Wildlife Sounds
National Sound Archive
29 Exhibition Road
London SW7 2AS
Tel: (01) 589 6603

If you are interested in recording the sounds of nature on tape, this is the Society for you. Its aims are to encourage the recording of wildlife sounds, to offer opportunities for technically improving recordings, and to promote the appreciation and understanding of animal language.

As a member you will be invited to two meetings each year. One meeting is in the autumn and a guest speaker is invited. The other meeting takes place over a spring weekend, when there is a chance to do some recording and swap ideas on equipment and technique. A tape of members' work is produced four times a year and sent round to members, and twice a year you will receive *Wildlife Sound*, a magazine full of interesting articles and reports. Also, there are three or four newsletters published each year, and two competitions are run, in which you can take part.

Apply to	the Honorary Secretary at the address above
Age range	older readers
Joining fee	none
Annual fee	B
Members	300
Date started	1968

Zoological Society of London (ZSL)

Regent's Park
London NW1 4RY
Tel: (01) 722 3333

A visit to a zoo can bring you face to face with animals and birds from every part of the world. If you live in or near London, and want to be close to wild animals so as to understand them and enjoy their beauty, then join the Zoological.

As a member of ZSL you can visit (free of charge) London Zoo and Whipsnade Park Zoo every day of the year except Christmas Day! You can take part in special events and activities, receive regular newsletters, and, if you want to take your friends along, they can pay less for their ticket.

By being a member you also help the zoos, which not only want to give their visitors an enjoyable day out, but also to study animals to find out how to help them in the wild. It plays an important role in breeding rare animals threatened with becoming extinct in the wild, due to the destruction of their habitat.

Apply to	Patsy Conway, at the address above
Age range	9–16
Joining fee	none
Annual fee	C
Members	7,535
Date started	1826

British Beekeepers' Association (BBKA)

National Agricultural Centre
Stoneleigh
Kenilworth
Warwickshire CV8 2LZ
Tel: (0203) 552404

A popular hobby is the care and management of swarms of honey-bees. Surprisingly, you do not have to live in the country to take part. Whether you live in a large city or in a village, you too can enjoy beekeeping and of course the honey the bees produce. If you want to find out more about taking up beekeeping this Association can help. Concerned with promoting beekeeping, the BBKA provides its members with meetings, training, information, the useful magazine *Bee Craft* each month, and a newsletter, *BBKA* four times a year.

Apply to	the General Secretary, at the address above
Age range	9–16
Joining fee	further information on request
Members	about 18,509
Date started	1874

British Trust for Ornithology (BTO)

Beech Grove
Tring
Hertfordshire HP23 5NR
Tel: (044 282) 3461

Watching birds can be a fascinating hobby. It's even more so when you can do this and help with important research into Britain's bird populations — mapping their distribution, tracing their patterns of migration, and identifying their habitats. By joining the Trust your hobby can help this major force in bird study. Since its earliest days the Trust has aimed to link amateurs and professionals so that their joint work can help our bird population.

Membership of the trust brings you a regular bulletin, *BTO News*, full of up-to-the-minute news, reviews, survey results, articles and information, together with the opportunity of receiving the two journals *Bird Study* and *Ringing and Migration* at greatly reduced prices. There is a variety of survey work in which you can take part, and your local Regional Representative will help you. Also there are national and regional birdwatchers' meetings; opportunities for grants and awards for your own research; specialist courses in ringing and census techniques; information and advice from the Trust's staff; occasional local meetings and newsletters; and the chance of using specialist library collections.

Membership of the Trust can clearly give you a lot, and at the same time you will know that you are helping to keep and develop its valuable fieldwork programme, analyse information gathered by surveys, and provide information for the conservation and protection of bird life.

Apply to	Mrs G. Bonham, at the address above
Age range	older readers
Joining fee	none
Annual fee	B
Members	8,000
Date started	1933

British Waterfowl Association (BWA)

c/o Mrs C.J. Winskill
6 Caldicott Close
Over
Winsford
Cheshire CW7 1LW
Tel: (0606) 594150

Ducks, geese and swans are kept by quite a few people, for no other purpose than they are good to look at. This Association is for those people who are keen about keeping, breeding and conserving all types of waterfowl, including wildfowl. Its work involves educating the public about waterfowl and the need for conservation, as well as raising the standards of keeping and breeding ducks, geese and swans in captivity.

As a member you receive twice a year the free magazine *Waterfowl* which has articles of general interest, advice on specific problems, book reviews, and information about shows and Open Days. Each year you will receive the *Water Fowl Yearbook and Buyers' Guide*; this includes articles and a big list of breeders with stock for sale. National Open Days are organised every year as are shows of domestic waterfowl so that you can visit some of the larger collections throughout the country. The Association can provide its members with advice and the opportunity to buy from a selection of books at reasonable prices.

Apply to	Mrs C.J. Winskill, at the address above
Age range	9–16
Joining fee	none
Annual fee	B
Members	1,400
Date started	1948

Irish Wildbird Conservancy (IWC)

Ruttledge House
8 Longford Place
Monkstown
Co Dublin
Ireland
Tel: (01) 804322

Almost 400 different species of wild birds have been recorded in Ireland; they range from common breeding birds and winter visitors to those rare breeds which arrive in the country by accident. There are laws which protect wild birds, but many are still under threat from illegal trapping, poisoning, shooting and oil pollution. The Irish Wildbird Conservancy works to protect birds and their natural habitats. It has a growing number of nature reserves which provide safety from man for all forms of wildlife. Through publications, films and events the Conservancy informs and educates people about birds and conservation. Surveys are made nationally to provide the facts which are important for conservation work.

If you join the IWC you will receive the quarterly magazine *IWC News*, containing lively articles, news and information on birds and birdwatching. Also, you can subscribe to *Irish Birds* published annually — essential reading for all birdwatchers in Ireland, and for all who take an interest in Irish birds. It is full of articles, reports of surveys and work undertaken by the Conservancy, together with book reviews, photographs, drawings and maps.

The IWC has a network of branches around the country. These arrange outings, talks and film shows. It also has national conferences, residential and one-day courses on birdwatching, chances to take part in surveys, and special outings and meetings for junior members — all provided by this, the largest organisation in Ireland devoted wholly to wild-life and conservation. Join now and have fun helping the IWC in its worthwhile work.

Apply to	Richard Nairn, at the address above
Age range	9–16
Joining fee	none
Annual fee	B
Members	over 4,000
Date started	1969

The Hawk Trust

c/o Bird of Prey Section
Zoological Society of London
Regent's Park
London NW1 4RY

Hawks, owls, eagles and falcons are to be found in Europe, the Americas, Asia, Africa and Australia. However, it is not certain that this will always be so; their natural habitats are being threatened by humans, and toxic chemicals threaten their position at the top of the food chain.

Although protected by law, birds of prey still suffer from illegal shooting, tapping, poisoning and nest-robbing. The Hawk Trust is dedicated to the conservation and appreciation of all birds of prey. If you join the Trust you can take part in field surveys of barn owls and martins, both under threat. Also you will be kept up-to-date by a newsletter issued twice a year describing the Trust's work.

Apply to	Mr Michael Walpole, 68 Outwoods Road, Loughborough, Leics, LE11 3LY
Age range	older readers
Joining fee	none
Annual fee	B
Members	475
Date started	1969

The Seabird Group

c/o RSPB
The Lodge
Sandy
Bedfordshire SG19 2DL
Tel: (0767) 80551

Finding out where there are seabird colonies, how large they are and which birds belong, is one of the present interests of The Seabird Group, which aims to bring together all those interested in the study of seabirds mainly in Britain and Ireland.

Anyone interested in seabirds can join. As a member you receive three newsletters a year which contain news, reports on research projects and details of meetings. *Seabird*, the group's magazine, is also sent free to members, who can benefit from the manuals and guidelines which the group publishes, and receive money to support some research. For example, the Group recently financed a census of gannet and roseate terns. Members are encouraged to take part in national surveys, such as the Beached Bird Survey and the National Site Register, which involves a lot of younger members.

Apply to	Dr E.K. Dunn, Dept of Zoology, South Parks Road, Oxford OX1 3PS
Age range	9–16
Joining fee	none
Annual fee	B
Members	330
Date started	1966

Scottish Ornithologists' Club (SOC)

21 Regent Terrace
Edinburgh EH7 5BT
Tel: (031) 556 6042

If you live in Scotland and have a serious interest in bird-watching, SOC is definitely the Club for you. Concerned with the study of Scottish bird life and the protection of rare birds, it has local branches throughout Scotland which organise winter lectures and field meetings. If you join SOC you will be a member of one of these branches, and receive *Scottish Birds*, a quarterly magazine containing articles, reports and reviews. There is an annual weekend conference at which it is possible to meet more than 300 members, take part in discussions, see films and listen to speakers from all over the world. You can take part in local and national surveys, and use possibly the best ornithological library in Scotland, the Waterston Library.

Apply to	Pat Webster, at the address above
Age range	9–16
Joining fee	none
Annual fee	B
Members	3,022
Date started	1936

Young Ornithologists' Club (YOC)

The Lodge
Sandy
Bedfordshire SG19 2DL
Tel: (0767) 80551

Most of the members of this Club are between nine and fourteen years old, although you can be a member up to sixteen years of age. The Club was formed to encourage bird-watching amongst young people. When you join you will receive a cloth arm-badge, a membership card, and the colour magazine *Bird Life* six times a year. This includes articles written by both expert bird-watchers and members, information about projects, and competitions. Each year there is a competition for different age groups to find three 'Young Ornithologists of the Year'.

You can take part in very popular holiday courses, some of which are based at youth hostels, and others at field centres. Also you can help with YOC projects. Recent ones have included a detailed report of summer migrants arriving in Britain, a survey of kestrels, a survey of garden birds, and a campaign to find and destroy discarded nylon fishing line and other fishing tackle. Each year members are asked to help in an annual National Sponsored Birdwatch. Funds from past years have been used to buy Fowlmere (an RSPB reserve), nestboxes, bird-tables and bird food for residential homes run by Dr Barnardo's, the National Children's Home and the Spastics Society, bird books for children's wards of hospitals, the special protection of red kites in Wales and rare birds breeding in Scotland, and improvements to an RSPB reserve so that handicapped visitors can visit and see and enjoy birds and other wildlife.

Maybe you have a brother or sister, or both, who would like to join YOC, too. If so, you pay a family membership, which is cheaper than your each paying individual membership.

Apply to	Mr Neil Morris, Promotions Officer, at the address above
Age range	9–16
Joining fee	none
Annual fee	B
Members	over 100,000
Date started	1965

Amateur Entomologists' Society (AES)

c/o 355 Hounslow Road
Hanworth
Feltham
Middlesex TW13 5JH
Tel: (01) 755 0325

AES was founded to promote the study of butterflies among amateurs, especially the young. If you join AES you are helped with your hobby through receiving the *Bulletin* four times a year; this includes articles written in a straightforward and easy to understand way, plus reports of what members have observed. A 'wants and exchanges list' is issued with the *Bulletin*, so that you can buy, sell or exchange equipment and so on. A Membership List helps you to make contact with other entomologists, and you can join special interest groups and benefit from the expert advice of an advisory panel, which helps with identification and other problems.

Each year an exhibition is held in London which you can visit; you can also go along to outdoor meetings to observe butterflies. Finally, the Society helps you to learn more about your hobby through its wide range of publications, including books, leaflets and pamphlets.

Apply to	The Registrar, at the address above
Age range	9–16
Joining fee	included in fee stated below
Annual fee	B
Members	1,750
Date started	1935

British Butterfly Conservation Society (BBCS)

Tudor House
102 Chaveney Road
Quorn
Nr Loughborough
Leicestershire LE12 8AD
Tel: (0509) 412870

There are at least nineteen types of butterfly threatened with extinction, seven being in particular danger. The BBCS aims to save or protect all types of British butterfly, either by conserving them in the wild or by breeding them in captivity and, where practicable, reintroducing them into natural habitats. The work of the Society falls into two areas — the detailed study of the nineteen endangered species, and a habitat survey.

It is the habitat survey in which as a member you can take part. You will discover how butterfly populations are affected by changes in habitat and the weather. This survey may produce extremely valuable information, at present almost completely lacking, on the needs of wild butterflies and ways of making sure they survive.

The Society organises meetings and exhibitions for members, and runs an information service. Four to six times a year you will receive *The News*, keeping you informed of the Society's work. A *Habitat Survey Guide* is also produced, which you can buy from the Society.

Apply to	Mrs L.M. Sutton, 19 Corner Close, Wellington, Somerset TA21 8QE
Age range	9–16
Joining fee	none
Annual fee	B
Members	2,736
Date started	1968

NOTES

8

Gardening

BONSAI

British Bonsai Association

Flat D
15 St John's Park
Blackheath
London SE3 7TH
Tel: (01) 677 9065

Bonsai is an interesting hobby in which you learn how to grow miniature trees. The trees you use are the ones you see around you, so they are not expensive. By using Bonsai techniques and skills, you can learn how to grow these trees in pots and to keep them small — small enough to sit on a balcony or on a patio.

If you join the British Bonsai Association, you can go to talks and demonstrations and to tree and pot sales, all held in London. You also receive a quarterly magazine about your hobby.

Apply to	the address above
Age range	9–16
Joining fee	B
Annual fee	A
Members	about 600
Date started	1974

CACTUS

British Cactus and Succulent Society (BCSS)

19 Crabtree Road
Botley
Oxford OX2 9DU
Tel: (0865) 248802

The BCSS caters for all levels of interest, from the professional botanist to the raw beginner with a few plants on the windowsill. As a member you will receive a magazine four times a year, full of excellent illustrations of cactus and other succulent plants. You will be able to get help with any problem in growing and propagating your plants, and in naming plants correctly. Advice is available on such subjects as soil mixtures, potting, pots, watering and heating. As seeds become available these are distributed to you.

In addition, a warm welcome awaits you at your local branch. In the United Kingdom there are more than 100 branches of the BCSS, grouped in geographical zones. As a new member you are attached to the branch of your own choice, usually the one nearest your home. Most branches hold monthly meetings, at which there may be illustrated lectures by invited speakers, a discussion, a quiz, and plant auctions. Usually there is a table show at the meeting, so you can exhibit your plants. Most branches also hold an annual show or exhibition, so that you can join in some fierce competition and show your best plants off to the public. Organised visits to nurseries, public and private collections and shows are also arranged. Many branches have a sales table at meetings for you to buy plants and horticultural sundries at reasonable prices, and to sell unwanted seedlings. The grouping of branches into zones makes it possible to join in inter-branch activities such as quizzes and shows. Some zones hold one-day conventions with speakers, and several publish excellent magazines.

Apply to	the address above
Age range	9–16
Joining fee	none
Annual fee	B
Members	5,500
Date started	1983

Good Gardeners' Association (GGA)

Arkley Manor Farm
Rowley Lane
Arkley
Barnet
Hertfordshire EN5 3HS

Interested in organic gardening? This Association gives information and advice about gardening using organic composts. It also discourages the use of insecticides and fungicides. At the Association's headquarters, Arkley Manor Farm Gardens, you can see organic gardening in action, and there are leaflets and books which you can buy.

Apply to	the address above
Age range	9–16
Joining fee	C
Annual fee	C
Members	400
Date started	1965

Royal Horticultural Society (RHS)

PO Box 313
80 Vincent Square
London SW1P 2PE
Tel: (01) 834 4333

When you join the RHS you get free admission to shows and lectures, to a special private view day at the famous Chelsea Flower Show, and to the Society's lovely garden at Wisley. You also get a colourful monthly magazine *The Garden*, full of articles, pictures and book reviews. You can borrow books from the Society's library. If you need advice, there are experts on hand to help in solving gardening problems and in identifying plants.

Apply to	the address above
Age range	9–16
Joining fee	none
Annual fee	B
Members	100,000
Date started	1804

Royal Horticultural Society of Ireland (RHSI)

Thomas Prior House
Merrion Road
Dublin 4

When you join the RHSI, you get free admission to illustrated talks, garden visits, shows, plant sales and some flower arranging demonstrations. You can also take part in garden tours, both at home and abroad, and borrow books from the Society's library.

Apply to	the address above
Age range	9–16
Joining fee	B
Annual fee	B
Members	1,200
Date started	1830

9

Outdoor Adventure

BACKPACKING

Backpackers' Club
20 St Michael's Road
Tilehurst
Reading
Berkshire RG3 4RP
Tel: (0734) 28754

Backpacking is an enjoyable, all-the-year-round way of life — the art of being totally independent for anything from short weekends to full annual holidays. Whether you are a lightweight walker, cyclist, canoeist or camper interested in this hobby, this Club is for you.

When you join Backpackers you can get information and advice from a special service, enjoy backpacking weekends from September to June, use the Foreign and Overseas Backpacking Travel Information Service, borrow from a lending library, and use the *Confidential Farm Pitch Directory* and the lists of long-distance footpaths, sites and pitches. Every three months you will receive the magazine *Back-pack*, full of interesting inform-ation. The Club also offers a camping equipment and personal effects insurance scheme. For a small price this covers the loss of, or damage to, your camping equipment.

In most counties the Club has an experienced member who advises on county meetings and activities, and help individual members. If you want to find out who your local representative is write to the Backpackers' Club, who will be pleased to help.

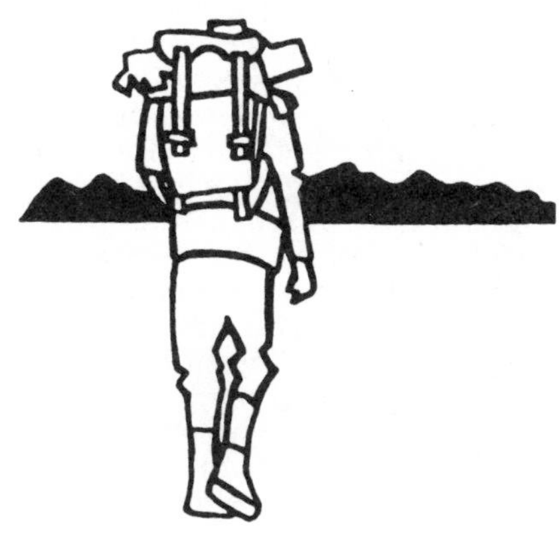

Apply to	Dr Eric R. Gurney, at the address above
Age range	older readers
Joining fee	further information on request
Members	9,000
Date started	1972

The Camping and Caravanning Club

11 Lower Grosvenor Place
London SW1W 0EY
Tel: (01) 828 1012/7

In early times people are known to have camped under tents of skins and leaves, but camping for fun is barely a hundred years old. Indeed, popular family camping began as recently as 1955. The first camping club in the world was begun by Thomas Hirain Holding in 1901, and eventually this club became known as The Camping and Caravanning Club. Tom Holding became its first president, followed by the famous names of Captain Robert Scott (the Antarctic explorer) and Lord Robert Baden-Powell (founder of the Scout movement).

Camping has a special appeal for young people. It gives independence, brings the pleasure of life outdoors, and introduces many new friends. But there is a lot more to camping than just buying a tent and a few bits of equipment and setting off for the countryside. *What* tent will best suit your needs? *How* do you know that you are getting value for money? *Where* should you pitch your tent when you have a whole field to choose from? *How* can you protect yourself from high winds and thunder-storms? This is where the Youth Section of this Club can help.

The Youth Section provides practical training to members, which leads to the award of a Certificate when you have passed the Youth Camping Test. For this test you learn the basic rules of camping and outdoor living.

The Youth Section also provides, between April and September of each year, organised activities in various parts of the country. Members can enjoy sports and activities such as orienteering, or simply the chance to meet new friends, lazing about the camp site. A party of members of the Youth Section travels to join the annual International Youth Rally held in a different European country each year; maybe you could join them? However, until you pass the Youth Camping Test, joining in these activities is limited by certain rules.

Once you have joined this Club, and the test has been passed, you can buy a copy of the Club's *Handbook and Sites List*, and subscribe to its monthly magazine *Camping and Caravanning*.

Apply to	Membership Dept, at the address above
Age range	12–16
Joining fee	none
Annual fee	B
Members	200,000
Date started	1901

National Caving Association (NCA)

Whernside Manor
Dent
Sedburgh
Cumbria LA10 5RE

If you are thinking of caving as a hobby you really ought to join a local club, and the NCA will give you the name and address of the person to contact in your area.

Apply to	the address above
Age range	older readers
Joining fee	paid by regional caving organisations
Annual fee	as above
Members	9 organisations
Date started	1969

British Mountaineering Council (BMC)

Crawford House
Precinct Centre
Booth Street East
Manchester M13 9RZ
Tel: (061) 273 5835

The sport of mountaineering, including hiking and climbing on rock, snow, and ice, began about 150 years ago, when English, French and German climbers, with their Swiss guides, first began to explore the mid-European Alps.

If you are interested in hill-walking, climbing on rock, snow, ice and artificial walls, alpinism and mountaineering expeditions, then the BMC is working for you. It calls for greater freedom of access to hills and crags, and for the conservation of mountain areas. It also sees that clothing and equipment for the hillwalker and climber are properly tested. If you join the BMC you support this work, but also benefit from the many services the Council has to offer.

There is a five day youngsters' training course, with instruction in basic techniques such as ropework, movement on rock and protection. Based at the Dartmoor Expedition Centre in Devon, it is run by the experienced climber John Earle and his wife. The BMC also organises climbing 'meets' each year in the United Kingdom and you can take part in these, as well as exchange visits abroad. Guidebooks and other publications, including the monthly magazine *High*, provide useful information. There are information sheets on clubs, huts, films, training courses and expedition planning, too. The Council offers insurance schemes specially designed for hillwalkers and climbers, and 'reciprocal rights cards' which let you hire alpine huts at discount rates.

Apply to	Ms Lesley Smithson, at the address above
Age range	9–16
Joining fee	none
Annual fee	B; D with magazine
Members	5,000
Date started	1944

Young Explorers' Trust (YET)

Royal Geographical Society
1 Kensington Gore
London SW7 2AR
Tel: (01) 589 9724

YET has over ten years' experience in advising people running expeditions. These may be anything from a weekend camp in Wales, to the ascent of a peak in the Himalayas, rebuilding tracks in the Lake District, or building schoolrooms in Papua New Guinea, surveying glaciers in Iceland or pushing wheelchairs up a hillside in Greece, digging wells in Africa or descending caves in Derbyshire. Whether you are able-bodied or handicapped you can benefit from the expedition experience: planning, running and taking part in an expedition uses and develops many personal qualities essential for normal living and working.

You can join YET either as an individual, or as a member of a school or youth club. The Trust advises on all aspects of planning expeditions, links members who run similar expeditions, organises seminars, lectures and other training and discussion meetings, publishes a bi-monthly magazine *YETMAG*, full of news, reports and informative articles, produces manuals and leaflets with practical advice, maintains study groups of members with common expedition interests, grants approval to expeditions which meet its standards of planning, and makes financial grants to many expeditions each year.

Apply to	Fiona Palmer, Administrative Officer, at the address above
Age range	older readers
Joining fee	none
Annual fee	D
Members	360
Date started	1970

The Girl Guides' Association (GGA)

17/19 Buckingham Palace Road
London SW1W 0PT
Tel: (01) 834 6242

Almost any interest can be followed and many new skills learned, including leadership and working as one of a team, when you join the Girl Guides' Association. If you are seven to ten years old you will join the Brownie Guides; if you are between ten and fifteen years, the Guides, and if between fourteen and eighteen years, the Ranger Guides. Handicapped girls have joined the Guides since the earliest days, and while there are special units, many are encouraged to join ordinary local units.

Two magazines are published for you by the association, *The Brownie* weekly, and *Today's Guide* monthly. In addition there are official handbooks, brochures, leaflets, charts, cassettes, and story and activity books, all about guiding.

At your meetings, once or twice a week and sometimes at weekends, there are badges to earn in such things as music, cookery and conservation. You may find yourself horseriding, camping, skating and acting. You can also take part in community and charity work and fund-raising. Increasingly there are joint activities which are jointly arranged with members of the Scout Association, and The Duke of Edinburgh's Award Scheme has a place in the training programme of both associations.

Write now and find where your nearest group meets.

Apply to	the address above
Age range	9–16
Joining fee	none
Annual fee	a small amount is paid each week
Members	850,708
Date started	1910

The Irish Girl Guides

Trefoil House
27 Pembroke Park
Dublin 4
Tel: (01) 683898

There are more than 900 units of The Irish Girl Guides throughout the twenty-six counties of Ireland. Girls of 6½ to 11 years may join the Brownie Branch and 10½ to 16 years the Guide Branch of this Association. When you join the Irish Girl Guides you will be able to learn a range of skills and win badges in a range of subjects from first aid to life saving, cookery to photography — there are ninety different badges in all. You will learn leadership and how to cope with responsibility. There are opportunities to go hiking and camping, and for making new friends. Why not write and find out where your nearest group meets?

Apply to	the Secretary-General, at the address above
Age range	9–16
Joining fee	none
Annual fee	B
Members	over 20,000
Date started	1930

The Scout Association
Baden-Powell House
Queen's Gate
London SW7 5JS
Tel: (01) 584 7030

There are nearly 12,000 Scout Groups in the United Kingdom, each with one or more Cub Scout Packs (8-11 years), one or more Scout Troups (11-16 years) and a Venture Scout Unit (16-20 years). As a member of the Scout Association you may find yourself camping, abseiling, climbing, canoeing, sailing, parascending, trekking, or taking part in Gang Shows, pantomimes or folk concerts. Some Scout Districts and Groups even have their own band. All members are kept in touch with news, developments and events in the Scouting movement through their monthly magazine *Scouting*.

A system of Progress Awards provides you with training goals in which the effort involved counts as much as the achievement. For Cubs the highest award is the Gold Arrow, for Scouts the Chief Scout's Award. As a Cub Scout you take part in games, sports and in learning by doing. You find out about the world and people around you, and become involved in raising money for charities and helping people in need. Scout Troops offer activities to match growing strength and widening interests. There is the chance to show initiative, and personal responsibility becomes important.

Why not join now? Write and find out where your nearest group meets.

Apply to	the Secretary, at the address above
Age range	9–16
Joining fee	none
Annual fee	varies between Groups
Members	16,477,417
Date started	1908

Ramblers' Association (RA)
1/5 Wandsworth Road
London SW8 2XX
Tel: (01) 582 6878

Whether you enjoy strolling along country paths or striding out on long-distance walks you ought to join the Ramblers' Association. Locally the RA guards the rights of way, making sure that there are paths for you to walk on. More than 250 local groups run working parties to keep the paths clear, build stiles and put up signposts and way-marks. Nationally, the RA is the walkers' pressure group; it is concerned with the law and policy plans affecting the countryside and your access to it.

When you join the RA you will be put into contact with a local group to walk with. Most of these groups run social events, too. Each year you will receive your free *Bed and Breakfast Guide* with more than 2,300 addresses where walkers are welcome, and four times a year the magazine *Rucksack*, plus your own area news. You will be able to use the 1:50,000 Ordnance Survey map library, and get discounts in more than a hundred outdoor equipment shops.

The RA produces free fact sheets on walking, and walking guides for all parts of Britain. You can also take up special offers on publications, as a discount subscription to *The Great Outdoors Magazine*. In addition to all of this you can call upon the national service of expert advice and information.

Apply to	the Membership Secretary, at the address above
Age range	9–16
Joining fee	none
Annual fee	B
Members	50,000
Date started	1935

Long Distance Walkers' Association (LDWA)

8 Upton Grey Close
Winchester
Hampshire SO22 6NE
Tel: (0256) 885356

If you enjoy walking long and very long distances — especially in rural, mountainous and moorland areas — this is the Association for you. The LDWA promotes organised challenge walks, pioneers new walking routes, and receives and publishes information on all aspects of non-competitive walking.

By 'long distance', the LDWA usually means distances of more than twenty miles (32km). Challenge walks organised include the Downsman Hundred, Malvern Midsummer Marathon and Ulf kil Stride. You have to achieve an objective (usually a set distance) within a time limit. Open challenge walks, such as the Three Peaks of Yorkshire, Lyke Wake Walk and Six Shropshire Summits, can be completed in any time.

Group walks are organised by local groups, of which there is a very strong network throughout the country. Other walks which you might take part in include walks along long distance footpaths and routes designed by the LDWA, for example, the Guildford Boundary and Bils dale Circuit, 'Kanters' (map-reading events organised by local groups), and marches (a series of one or more day walks).

If you join the LDWA you not only get the chance to go on some of these walks, but also three times a year you will receive the magazine *Strider*, which includes details of all major walks, reports on past events, a calendar of future events, maps, photographs, letters and reviews of books.

Apply to	Mr E. Bishop, Lodgefield Cottage, High Street, Flimwell, Wadhurst, East Sussex, TN5 7PA
Age range	older readers
Joining fee	none
Annual fee	B
Members	4,075
Date started	1971

Youth Hostel Association
Trevelyan House
8 St Stephen's Hill
St Albans
Hertfordshire AL1 2DY
Tel: (0727) 55215

The YHA is a worldwide club offering you the chance to get away and combine adventure and leisure. You can discover both England and abroad at reasonable prices, thanks to the YHA.

With its network of 260 youth hostels in England and Wales, there is a good range of places to stay, including a ghostly Norman castle and an elegant Georgian mansion. Whether you visit a city, the countryside, or the seaside there is usually a hostel close by, and always you will find a warm welcome awaiting you. A night's stay costs about £3, and low-cost meals and snacks are provided; alternatively you can cater for yourself. You sleep in bunk-bedded rooms or dormitories or, if you are holidaying with your family, you may have a private family room.

If you want to travel abroad the YHA has over 5,000 hostels in more than fifty countries, and the YHA card can get you cheap travel to many foreign countries. The YHA also runs its own travel services, which helps with tickets and reservations both in England and abroad.

The YHA also organises a programme of action-packed breaks for all kinds of activities including walking, pot-holing, pony-trekking and canoeing.

If you prefer something less energetic you can choose from activities such as art, bird-watching and fossil-hunting. Experts are at hand to help, and so is any equipment you may need.

There are over a hundred local YHA groups throughout the country. They organise not only social meetings and hostelling trips, but also summer barbecues, bonfire parties, cycle runs, conservation projects and film shows.

When you join the YHA you will be sent a *Guide*, and a map for handy pocket reference. The *Guide* includes a full description of each hostel and its facilities, lists local attractions including steam railways and historic buildings. It also includes booking forms, maps and other useful information. Four times a year you will receive the *YHA Magazine* full of news and ideas.

Apply to	the address above
Age range	9–16
Joining fee	none
Annual fee	5–15 A; 16 B; if you are under 16 and your parents are members — free
Members	a quarter of a million
Date started	1930

Scottish Youth Hostels Association (SYHA)

7 Glebe Crescent
Stirling FK8 2JA
Tel: (0786) 51181

As with the YHA and the YHA of NI, this Association provides hostels equipped with kitchens, common room and dormitories, offering low-cost holidays. If you *live* in Scotland you can join this Association, but if you wish to *visit* Scotland then a membership card for your own country's YHA will let you use the Scottish hostels. Each year a SYHA *Handbook* and a touring map are published by the Association, and are very valuable to hostelling visitors.

The SYHA also organises Breakaway holidays, which include pony-trekking at Loch Ard in the Trossachs and Snoot in the Borders, canoeing on Loch Lomond and Loch Lochy, sailing on the sea at Tighnabruaich or on the inland lochs near Aviemore, walking, exploring the mountains and glens of the West Coast and Central Highlands, and mountaincroft climbing in Glencoe, Glen Nevis, or the Cairngorms at Loch Morlich. There are also SYHA ski schools at Braemar and Loch Morlich.

Apply to	Fiona Kerr, at the address above
Age range	9–16
Joining fee	none
Annual fee	5–15 A; 16+ B
Members	45,745
Date started	1932

Youth Hostel Association of Northern Ireland (YHANI)

56 Bradbury Place
Belfast BT7 1RU
Tel: (0232) 324733

Like the YHA this Association provides low-cost accommodation in all kinds of places from castles and country houses to simple cottages, situated at the seaside, on mountains, in cities, by forests and lakeshores, all in Northern Ireland. Your membership card will let you use hostels throughout the world, and advice on these can be obtained from the YHANI. It also organises a range of low-cost cycling, rambling and touring holidays in Northern Ireland.

Apply to	the Secretary, at the address above
Age range	9–16
Joining fee	none
Annual fee	B, and a stamped self-addressed envelope
Members	7,500
Date started	1931

Stirling Youth Hostel

NOTES

10

Pressure Groups

ANIMAL RIGHTS

Beauty Without Cruelty (BWC)

11 Lime Hill Road
Tunbridge Wells
Kent TN1 1LJ
Tel: (0892) 25587

Did you know that, to see if lipsticks, hairdyes and face powders are safe for humans, they are force-fed to animals to see how much they eat before being poisoned? That shampoos and lotions are dropped into rabbits' eyes, sometimes forced open for days on end? Or that to make one fur coat six to twelve cheetahs, three to five leopards, or thirty to sixty-five mink may have to die? And that thousands of seal pups are shot or clubbed to death, when seven to ten days old, so that their pelts can be made into fur coats?

If these facts concern you, Beauty Without Cruelty — an international educational charity with branches throughout Britain — would like your support as a member. You will receive a newsletter, informative leaflets aimed at young people, and a twice-yearly magazine, *Compassion*. Also, you will know that your support is helping BWC to tell people about the suffering of animals, and show them that there are alternatives for the manufacture of furs, cosmetics and toiletries.

Apply to	Membership Secretary, at address above
Age range	9–16
Joining fee	none
Annual fee	B
Date started	1959

The Farm and Food Society

4 Willifield Way
London NW11 7XT
Tel: (01) 455 0634

Farming is essential to our survival, but need it also be cruel to animals and harmful to ourselves and the environment? This Society thinks not. It encourages farming which is humane to animals, provides wholesome food, and combines the best traditional methods with the wise use of technology. In other words, better and safer food, happier animals, less pollution and more conservation. Membership is worldwide, and the Society has a high reputation, advising the government and the media.

Through letters and articles in the press it informs the public of its aims and work. Members receive an *Annual Report*, and a quarterly newsletter describing current activities and international developments, and including book reviews and conference reports. Why not join now and help this Society in its work for better farming?

Apply to	the address above
Age range	older readers
Joining fee	none
Annual fee	B
Date started	1966

National Society Against Factory Farming (NSAFF)

41 Mercator Road
Lewisham
London SE13 5EH
Tel: (01) 852 1832

Do you know that hens, calves, pigs, rabbits, turkeys, partridges, pheasants, geese and red deer are amongst the many animals and birds factory-farmed in Britain? This type of farming is considered to be one way of providing cheap and plentiful food, but it can mean suffering for the animals and birds. Instead of living out of doors, they are often housed in cramped sheds. Hens are kept in cages too small for them to move around; pigs are reared in total darkness; veal calves can't even turn around or lie down properly because their stalls are so small.

This Society aims to stop this suffering, and works to bring an end to factory farming. If you join NSAFF your subscription will help it to tell people about the poor conditions in factory farms, to take those farmers who do not provide good conditions to court, and to work for improvements. You will receive a regular newsletter and information on where to buy food which is *not* factory-farmed. You can also help NSAFF by raising funds and recruiting new members.

Apply to	Mrs L.J. Newman, at the address above
Age range	older readers
Annual fee	B
Members	5,000
Date started	not known

Chickens' Lib

PO Box 2
Holmfirth
Huddersfield HD7 1QT
Tel: (0484) 861814

The factory-farming of chickens is the sole concern of this group, which works for the end of the battery-cage system for laying hens, and campaigns for free range eggs. There are around forty million battery hens in this country today. They are confined in gloomy foul-smelling sheds in cages roughly eight inches by eight inches square; here they will spend up to two years standing or crouching on a sloping wire floor. These are just some of the facts that Chickens' Lib makes known to its members through fact sheets and a regular newsletter. When you join you are sent copies of all fact sheets, and the latest issue of the Newsletter. This is a strictly non-violent group, which tells the public about the distress caused to chickens by battery farming. If you share the group's concern, then find out more by writing to Chickens' Lib.

Apply to	the address above
Age range	older readers
Joining fee	none
Annual fee	B
Members	970
Date started	1973

British Hedgehog Preservation Society (BHPS)

Knowbury House
Knowbury
Ludlow
Shropshire SY8 3LQ
Tel: (0584) 890287

This Society encourages the fitting of escape-ramps in all cattle and sheep grids; this saves the hedgehog's life, as it would otherwise die of lack of food and water. It educates people to appreciate and respect all our natural wildlife, particularly hedgehogs, and pays for research into the behaviour of hedgehogs. There is a healthy and growing membership, which regularly receives a newsletter.

The Society deals with many hundreds of queries from the public about how to care for hedgehogs, and has published (with the RSPCA) a very useful pamphlet on hedgehogs. To help raise money for research, it also sells many articles such as sweat shirts and teeshirts, aprons, cards and other novelties all decorated with hedgehogs.

So, by joining this Society, you not only get to know more about hedgehogs and help to keep them as part of our national heritage, but also can solve some of your birthday and Christmas present problems!

Apply to	Major A.H. Coles, at the address above
Age range	9–16
Joining fee	none
Annual fee	B
Members	4,650
Date started	1982

British Trust for Conservation Volunteers (BTCV)

36 St Mary's Street
Wallingford
Oxfordshire OX10 0EU
Tel: (0491) 39766

This Trust brings together people, tools and equipment, careful organisation and energy into a unique workforce, dedicated to meet the desperate needs of our rural and urban landscape. Volunteers work to protect nature and wildlife from the many threats of modern living — destruction, neglect, disease or over-use. By joining the Trust you can get involved. There are more than 400 conservation working holidays organised throughout the United Kingdom lasting one or two weeks. There is also a daily programme of projects run from BTCV offices in most towns and cities in England, Wales and Northern Ireland. Trees are being planted; wasteland sites are cleared and made into nature gardens or tree nurseries; clogged-up ponds and streams are cleaned and footpaths cleared; drystone walls are repaired. Four times a year you will receive *The Conserver*, a magazine which will keep you in touch with the work of the Trust, through news, features and information.

Apply to	Mr David Aston, at the address above
Age range	9–16
Joining fee	none
Annual fee	B
Members	40,000
Date started	1970

Council for the Protection of Rural Wales (CPRW)

Ty Gwyn
31 High Street
Welshpool
Powys SY21 7JP
Tel: (0938) 2525

Living in Wales and worried about damage to the Welsh countryside? Concerned about unsuitable building development and road schemes, unsightly caravan parks, and damaging mineral-mining? Worried about the closing of post offices and schools and the removal of telephone kiosks, and the run down of local transport?

These are the concern of the Council, which tries to stop undesirable development. It seeks to improve the amenities of rural life, supports realistic conservation, and balances the demands of commercial interest with those of the protection of the environment. As a member of the CPRW you can join a local branch and take an active part in its work. You will receive the magazine *Rural Wales*, and be able to attend special study conferences for young people.

Apply to	Mr Simon Meade, Director, at the address above
Age range	older readers
Joining fee	none
Annual fee	B
Members	about 3,000
Date started	1928

Friends of the Earth Limited (FOE)

377 City Road
London EC1V 1NA
Tel: (01) 837 0731

According to Friends of the Earth, our world is under threat — by nuclear and toxic wastes, pesticides, acid rain, asbestos, destruction of wildlife, countryside and tropical rain forests, depletion and misuse of natural resources, and the waste of unemployment. FOE is a non party-political, national pressure group with 250 action groups. It tells people how to protect their environment, lobbies politicians, and presses for changes in the law and in national and local government policies.

As a Friend of the Earth you can join a local group and attend its meetings. You receive a regular newspaper containing detailed information on the work of FOE campaigns, as well as a wide range of information sheets. There are also conferences and workshops for you to go to, and campaigns in which you can take a part, helping to make this a better, more caring world in which to live.

Apply to	Sherna Chatterjee, at the address above
Age range	older readers
Joining fee	none
Annual fee	B
Members	18,000
Date started	1971

Irish Environmental Conservation Organisation for Youth – UNESCO CLUBS (ECO-UNESCO Clubs)

The Tailors Hall
Back Lane
Dublin 8
Ireland
Tel: (01) 783940

For those of you living in Ireland, with an interest in and concern for your environment, this voluntary national youth movement offers a chance to take part in activities dealing with issues such as threats to wildlife, air and water pollution, litter and recycling, and the use of natural resources. ECO promotes information, training and action to conserve and develop our natural and cultural heritage, and through 'learning by doing' you can help to improve your local surroundings. Local Eco-Unesco Clubs plan and carry out their own action programmes, and you can take part in this community based work, and work-away weekend and summer camps.

Apply to	the Membership Secretary, at the address above
Age range	9–16
Joining fee	none
Annual fee	B (B for up to 4 children of same family living at one address)
Members	16,000
Date started	1982

Men of the Trees (MOTT)

Crawley Down
Crawley
Sussex RH10 4HL
Tel: (0342) 712536

According to the Men of the Trees, trees are the only insurance against soil erosion which makes deserts and wastelands; it is trees that hold the soil together. They also provide shelter for livestock and crops, maintain the water table, take in vast quantities of carbon dioxide and give off almost pure oxygen. Without enough trees many thousands of birds, insects, plants and animals will become extinct.

The Men of the Trees is an international organisation actively concerned with improving our environment — with the beauty of our parks, natural woodlands and forests, and with the direct link between food production and trees, particularly in developing countries. By joining the Men of the Trees you can support their work in saving, protecting and planting trees. On joining you will receive a New Members Pack, which contains details of the Society's activities (local and worldwide), a large colour poster, the publication *Tree Story*, a car sticker and a free packet of tree seeds. Meetings and exhibitions are held which you can go to, and twice a year you will receive the magazine *Trees*.

Apply to	Mrs E. Sandwell, National Secretary, at the address above
Age range	9–16
Joining fee	none
Annual fee	B
Members	3,650
Date started	1922

Landlife

Urban Wildlife Unit
131 Mount Pleasant
Liverpool L3 5TF
Tel: (051) 709 1013

Landlife is concerned that now, more than ever before, the beautiful landscape of Britain is under threat. Wildlife areas are being destroyed and Landlife looks at ways of making new habitats for plants and animals. Landlife welcomes members to support their work which includes reclaiming land, running a wildflower nursery, undertaking major nature conservation surveys, and telling the public about the need to protect wildlife.

When you join Landlife you will receive a membership package including a 64-page workbook, *The School Garden Book*, which can be used either at school or in your own garden, the *Natterjack* magazine, *Landlife News*, a butterfly badge, and a set of re-usable labels. Both *Natterjack* and *Landlife News* will continue to be sent to you as long as you are a member.

Apply to	Gillian Watson, Membership Secretary, at the address above
Age range	9–16
Joining fee	none
Annual fee	B
Members	200
Date started	1975

Open Spaces Society

25A Bell Street
Henley-on-Thames
Oxfordshire RG9 2BA
Tel: (0491) 573535

The Open Spaces Society claims that 1½ million acres of common land, together with town and village greens throughout England and Wales, are being destroyed; many of the 100,000 miles of country paths and green lanes are being obstructed, ploughed up or closed. If you join Open Spaces you can support work to rescue threatened open space and save the footpaths and bridleways from being obstructed and destroyed. Three times a year you will receive the magazine, *Open Space*, which is full of information, and be able to buy at lower prices any of the Society's publications. It is surprising to see that the Society was founded in 1865, and that sadly over a hundred years later there is still a need to protect our open spaces.

Apply to	the Membership Secretary, at the address above
Age range	older readers
Joining fee	none
Annual fee	B
Members	3,000
Date started	1865

The National Trust

36 Queen Anne's Gate
London SW1H 9AS
Tel: (01) 222 9251

The name National Trust may bring to mind the preservation of country houses and their contents, but in fact the Trust preserves — besides its 250 historic buildings — gardens and landscaped parks, countryside, woods and downland, lakes, mountains, coastline, prehistoric and Roman sites, relics of our industrial past, over a thousand farms, forty traditional villages and hamlets, and even eighteen dovecotes!

When you join the National Trust you will receive a card which gives you free admission to an ever-growing list of properties, a colour magazine *National Trust* three times a year, the members' handbook, and a 240-page guide telling you where to visit National Trust properties. Join now, and start exploring your national heritage.

Apply to	the Membership Secretary, at the address above
Age range	older readers
Joining fee	none
Annual fee	C
Members	1,322,996
Date started	1895

The Orang-Utan Conservation Project

22 Cherry Arbor
Cressage
Near Shrewsbury
Shropshire
Tel: (095289) 762

This worthwhile conservation project desperately needs more members to help in its important work. The orang-utan has been an endangered species for some time, but only recently has it been seen how rare this animal is becoming. Today it is found in the wild only on two islands of Indonesia, Sumatra and Borneo. With large-scale logging of the rainforest in these areas, its numbers are very much threatened. Without careful discussion and planning between the lumber companies, the Indonesian Government, and concerned scientists the orang-utan could disappear forever.

This project raises money in Britain for the Orang-Utan Research and Conservation Project in Borneo. The Borneo centre was set up to protect and study wild orang-utans and their habitat. The project is based in the Tanjung Puting Reserve in Central Kalimantan, Borneo.

By sending money to this project you will be helping its work. Everyone sending money is sent copies of all of the publications produced by the project, and it is hoped soon to include a newsletter with these

Apply to	Mrs Gill Gannon, at the address above
Age range	9–16
Joining fee	none
Annual fee	none
Date started	1984

Rare Breeds Survival Trust Limited (RBST)

4th Street
National Agricultural Centre
Kenilworth
Warwickshire CV8 2LG
Tel: (0203) 696551

During the first seventy-three years of this century at least twenty breeds of British farm livestock have died out. More than forty breeds are now receiving support from this Trust, because their numbers are so small that their continued existence cannot be taken for granted. A large number of these threatened breeds — for example Gloucester cattle and Cotswold sheep — were popular less than thirty years ago. The Trust works to ensure that no more breeds die out. It believes that there will come a time when farming will need these rare breeds to improve the narrow range of animals bred at present. If you join the Trust you will support its work, and receive *The Ark*, a monthly magazine full of news, views, for sale and wanted advertisements for rare breeds, features, letters and notices of shows where you can see rare breeds.

Apply to	Mrs Betty Wilkinson, at the address above
Age range	all ages
Joining fee	none
Annual fee	C
Members	over 7,000
Date started	1973

Ulster Society for the Preservation of the Countryside (USPC)

West Winds
Carney Hill
Holywood
County Down BT18 0JR
Tel: (0232) 661222

If you live in Ulster and value the heritage of natural beauty, and if you have ever seen a favourite spot of the countryside in danger of being spoiled and wondered what you could do about it, this is *your* Society, and one which will help you to put things right. The USPC recognises the urgent need to care for and protect the natural environment of Ulster against the pressures of today. It is a public watchdog, dealing with such things as rights of way, the protection of trees, the dumping of rubbish, mining concessions, the control of quarrying, and the siting of motorways.

As a member of USPC you support this important work, and can go to a series of winter lectures in Queen's University. Walks and excursions are made in Spring to places of scenic, historic and preservation interest, and you can take part in these. You will receive in spring and autumn, a magazine, *The Countryside Recorder*.

Apply to	Mr Wilfrid Capper, Honorary Secretary, at the address above
Age range	older readers
Joining fee	none
Annual fee	B
Members	500
Date started	1937

Watch Trust for Environmental Education Limited (WATCH)

22 The Green
Nettleham
Lincoln LN2 2NR
Tel: (0522) 752326

WATCH is a club with a difference for young people who care about their surroundings in town and country. If you join WATCH you will receive three times a year an exciting magazine *Watchword*, full of pictures, puzzles, information and ideas for things to do. You will

also get a newsletter from your local WATCH group. Every year there are new surveys and projects to take part in, and you might get a badge or win a prize or certificate if you do. An example of a past project is the national survey of acid rain, in which more than 2,000 youngsters took part. Local activities include interesting projects with names such as beach-combing, hedgerow harvest, fungal foray and creepy crawlies. Join WATCH, and learn about your surroundings, have fun and make friends.

Apply to	the Membership Secretary, at the address above
Age range	9–16
Joining fee	none
Annual fee	B (C for 3 years); B per family of up to 4 children living at one address (C for 3 years)
Members	16,800
Date started	1977

National Campaign for Firework Reform

15, 118 Long Acre
London WC2E 9PA
Tel: (01) 836 6703

This campaign was started by groups of parents concerned about the terrible injuries caused by fireworks to children and young people. The campaign wants laws to limit fireworks to holders of licences, and particularly for properly organised firework displays. In 1985 it inaugurated the Beverley Pentland Safety Certificate Award for the best safety at organised firework displays; this is awarded at a special ceremony each year. If you join this campaign you will help it in its work to make fireworks safer, and will receive information sheets, newsletters, the *International Firework Report*, and other leaflets to keep you informed.

Apply to	Noël Tobin, Director, at the address above
Age range	9–16
Joining fee	none
Annual fee	none
Members	25,015
Date started	1969

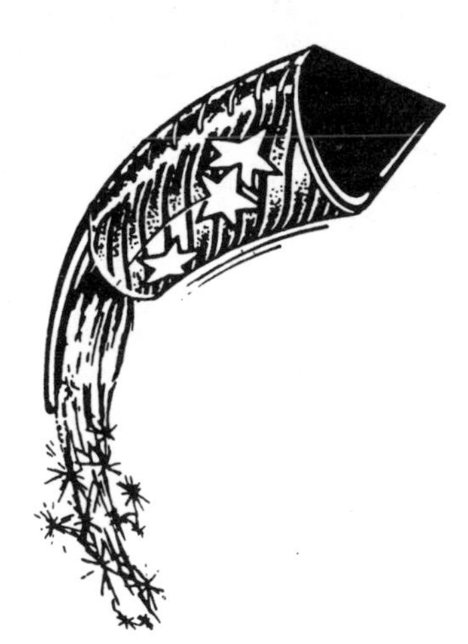

Amnesty International British Section

5 Roberts Place
Off Bowling Green Lane
London EC1R 0EJ
Tel: (01) 251 8371

This important organisation seeks the release of prisoners of conscience. These are men and women imprisoned anywhere in the world because of their beliefs, colour, sex, ethnic origin, language or religion, and who have neither used nor advocated violence. A.I. also calls for fair and early trials for all political prisoners and works on behalf of such people detained without charge or trial. A.I. also opposes the death penalty and torture of prisoners. In 1977 it was awarded the Nobel Peace Prize for its work, followed in 1978 by the United Nations Human Rights Prize.

Today A.I. has thousands of members in more than 150 countries, and by joining you help to support its work. You can even join or start an Amnesty Group in your school; A.I. will give lots of ideas for club activities which will help its work, including raising funds and helping to campaign on behalf of prisoners.

Apply to	Gillian Ball, at the address above
Age range	older readers
Joining fee	none
Annual fee	B
Members	350,000
Date started	1961

Anti-Apartheid Movement

13 Mandela Street
London NW1 0DW
Tel: (01) 387 7966

This movement came about after Africa's first Nobel Peace Prize winner, Chief Albert Luthuli, called for a boycott of South Africa because it practises apartheid, or racial segregation. It organises meetings, rallies, pickets, exhibitions and film shows to publicise the facts about apartheid in South Africa and Namibia, and to campaign for its end. There are over 120 local groups in most large towns and cities throughout the country; a Scottish Committee coordinates activities in Scotland. In Wales, action is organised by the Welsh Anti-Apartheid Movement.

When you join you will receive *Anti-Apartheid News* ten times a year, a members' newsletter giving up-to-date information on local and national action against apartheid, and information on developments in South Africa. If you believe in freedom in Southern Africa then join this movement.

Apply to	Mamta Singh, at the address above
Age range	older readers
Joining fee	none
Annual fee	B
Members	31,600
Date started	1959

Anti-Slavery Society

180 Brixton Road
London SW9 6AT
Tel: (01) 582 4040

Most people think that slavery is a thing of the past, but sadly, this is not so. Millions of children are still abused as they were in the 19th century; often, they are forced to work in conditions as terrible as in the factories of 150 years ago. Did you know there are still nine-year-old coal miners, little girls who work twelve-hour shifts in factories, and small children abandoned to live by their wits in city streets? According to this Society, in Thailand, India, Morocco, Italy, South Africa and many other countries children are exploited as cheap and obedient labour.

The Anti-Slavery Society speaks out for these children, and others who suffer various forms of slavery. It tells the public about their plight and campaigns for the abolition of slavery and child labour. You can help by joining this Society and getting to know the facts from its publications, its magazine *Anti-Slavery Reporter*, and newsletters; by supporting specific campaigns; and by encouraging others to join.

Apply to	the Deputy Director, at the address above
Age range	older readers
Joining fee	none
Annual fee	B
Members	1,012
Date started	1839

Campaign for Nuclear Disarmament (CND)

22-24 Underwood Street
London N1 7JG
Tel: (01) 250 4010

CND is not only concerned that nuclear weapons exist, but that money badly needed for other things is being spent on them. For example, CND believes that for the cost of Trident — Britain's new nuclear weapon — 500 new hospitals could be built. CND also believes that far from making us feel safe, the world's 50,000 nuclear weapons are creating greater fear and insecurity, and that these weapons eat up huge sums of money, skills and resources which could be better used.

CND believes in dismantling nuclear weapons in Britain, and setting an example for the rest of the world to follow. If you want to support this work, then you can join now. You will be put in touch with your local group, and get information about CND's work.

Apply to	Alison Williams, at address above
Age range	older readers
Joining fee	none, but a donation is requested
Annual fee	A
Members	110,000
Date started	1958

NOTES

11

Sports

Association for Archery in Schools (AAS)

Bloxham School
Banbury
Oxfordshire OX15 4PE
Tel: (0295) 720443

If you are already in a junior archery club, maybe at school, and this club belongs to the AAS there is a lot of enjoyment ahead of you. The AAS is connected to the Grand National Archery Society, and promotes archery in schools and junior clubs. Being in a club means that you can take part in the Achievement Badge Scheme, which will help you to reach almost Junior Master Bowman standard. You can also enter the British Schools Archery Championship and various other tournaments, use special rounds and handicapping for age, sex and bow-type so that everyone has a chance to take part. These competitions have separate team events for school and non-school clubs. The AAS also organises summer and winter postal leagues for club teams of four archers. Coaching events are sometimes held, and details of this and other events are sent to member clubs once a term.

If your club is *not* a member of AAS, tell its organiser what you are all missing!

If you are thinking about taking up archery and do not yet belong to a club, the AAS will tell you where your nearest affiliated club meets, and whom to contact.

Apply to	Mr C. Fletcher-Campbell, at the address above
Age range	9–16
Joining fee	none
Annual fee	C
Members	128
Date started	1963

Grand National Archery Society (GNAS)

7th Street
National Agricultural Centre
Stoneleigh
Kenilworth
Warwickshire CV8 2LG
Tel: (0203) 23907

GNAS is the governing body for archery in Great Britain and Northern Ireland. It is through this Society that archery is included in the Olympic games, World and European Championships, and international tournaments.

The Society is divided into nine regional societies. Each of these organises annual championships and open tournaments in all types of archery — target, field, clout, flight and indoor — for both senior and junior members. National tournaments are organised too. Both boys and girls are welcome as members, as are young people with physical handicaps.

If you are thinking of taking up archery then this Society can offer useful advice on joining a local club, costs, and buying equipment. Once you have grasped the basics you can start practising for the many badges and medals the Society awards.

You can join GNAS as an individual, by being a member of a club connected with it, or through the Association for Archery in Schools. As a member you will receive *News from the Centre*, a magazine produced by the Society six times a year.

Apply to	Mr J.J. Bray, at the address above
Age range	9–16
Joining fee	none
Annual fee	D individual membership
Members	16,954
Date started	1861

Amateur Athletic Association (AAA)

Francis House
Francis Street
London SW1P 1DL
Tel: (01) 828 9326

If you are in an athletics club this is a worthwhile Association for your club to join. The aim of the AAA is to control, promote and provide athletic competitions, coaching and training. It does these by providing its members (which are clubs) with meetings, training, proficiency examinations, competitions, a series of instructional booklets, and a useful information service.

Young athletes in school clubs in England, Wales and Northern Ireland, which are also members of the AAA, can take part in the 5-Star Proficiency Scheme, open to girls and boys. They can also win certificates for their athletic performance. The AAA includes a section for disabled athletes, and their clubs are welcome as members, too.

If you are not a member of a club, but would like to find out where your nearest AAA club meets, write to the AAA and ask.

Apply to	the address above
Age range	9–16
Joining fee	none
Annual fee	paid by clubs
Members	1,300 clubs
Date started	1880

English Schools' Athletic Association (ESAA)

26 Conniscliffe Road
Stanley
County Durham DH9 7RF
Tel: (0207) 232507

Schools who want to encourage their pupils in athletics probably already belong to their county's schools athletic association; these associations can be members of the ESAA. Membership means that you can benefit from the ESAA's expert advice on organising athletic events, and take part in yearly national cross-country, track and field, and race-walking championships. There are international matches, too. You can also take part in the ESAA Milk in Action Award Scheme for school children. When you have reached a certain level of skill in an event such as long jump, discus and steeplechase, you will qualify for a special badge. Does your school belong to this Association? Find out — you could be missing a lot of fun!

Apply to	Mr N. Dickinson, at the address above
Age range	9–16
Joining fee	none
Annual fee	paid by county association
Members	46 county associations
Date started	1925

Northern Ireland Women's Amateur Athletic Association (NIWAAA)

112 Orangefield Crescent
Belfast BT6 9GJ
Tel: (0232) 704891

The aim of this Association is to promote women's amateur athletics events in Northern Ireland. If you belong to an athletics club in Northern Ireland which is a member of the NIWAAA you can take part in the competitions it organises. If you don't, it will be pleased to tell you which of its member clubs meets near you, and then you too can take part.

Apply to	Mrs Adrienne Smyth, Honorary Secretary, at the address above
Age range	further information on request
Joining fee	as above
Annual fee	as above
Members	17 clubs

Scottish Amateur Athletic Association (SAAA)

18 Ainslie Place
Edinburgh EH3 6AU
Tel: (031) 226 4401

If you live in Scotland and want to take part in athletics, the SAAA can give you information about clubs in your area. Once you have joined you can take part in competitions and other events organised by the SAAA.

Apply to	Mr J.D. Fairgrieve, Administrator, at the address above
Age range	11–16
Joining fee	Paid for by clubs
Annual fee	as above
Members	5,300
Date started	1883

Scottish Cross-Country Union (SCCU)

18 Ainslie Place
Edinburgh EH3 6AU
Tel: (031) 226 4401

Scottish clubs and schools who want to promote and develop cross-country running can join this Union, which aims to encourage cross-country running in Scotland. The union promotes competitions in which you can take part, and helps in the award of the George Dallas Memorial Trophy each year; this is awarded to the person, or persons, who has/have achieved distinction, or made some other contribution to cross-country running in Scotland. There is also a George Dallas Memorial Fund, which aims to help young Scottish athletes by making money available each year to assist in training, coaching, travelling and provide equipment.

If you live in Scotland and your club or school is interested in cross-country running, see if it has joined this Union. If you would like to join a club, and wonder where your nearest club is, the union should be able to tell you.

Apply to	Mr J.E. Clifton, 8 Craigshannoch Road, Wormit, Fife, DD6 8ND
Age range	9–16
Joining fee	none
Annual fee	paid by school or club
Members	131 schools and clubs
Date started	1890

Scottish Schools' Athletic Association (SSAA)

11 Muirfield Street
Kirkcaldy
Fife KY2 6SY
Tel: (0592) 260168

If you live in Scotland and your school is a member of this Association, you can take part in annual national school championships; events include road relay, cross-country running, pentathlon and relay, plus track and field events. There are also international events each year in cross-country and track and field, in which you might be able to take part. The SSAA holds meetings and provides an information service for its members, and publishes a year book, a list of members and a yearly report, all sent free to members. Ask if your school is a member of SSAA, because *you* could have a chance to train for and compete in these exciting events.

Apply to	Mr A. Jack, Secretary, at the address above
Age range	9–16
Joining fee	none
Annual fee	paid by schools
Members	500 schools
Date started	1934

Scottish Women's Amateur Athletic Association (SWAAA)
18 Ainslie Place
Edinburgh EH3 6AU
Tel: (031) 226 4401

SWAAA promotes athletics for women in Scotland, and organises competitions and coaching open to young people.

Apply to	Mr J.D. Fairgrieve, Administrator, at the address above
Age range	9–16
Joining fee	paid for by clubs
Annual fee	as above
Members	about 80 clubs
Date started	1934

Badminton Association of England (BA of E)
National Badminton Centre
Bradwell Road
Loughton Lodge
Milton Keynes
Buckinghamshire MK8 9LA
Tel: (0908) 568822

Schools, clubs and youth associations can all join this Association, which aims to promote badminton in England, the Channel Islands and the Isle of Man. It is this Association which makes the rules under which tournaments and championships are played.

If you belong to a member club you can take part in the English National Junior Championships. The W Wiltshire Coaching Scholarship is awarded each year to a promising junior player who, in the opinion of the Coaching and Technical Committee, could benefit from some special coaching.

Badminton News, the Association's magazine, is sent to clubs ten times a year, free of charge. It includes news, photographs, tournament and competition reports, letters and other interesting reading. Find out if your school or club is a member of BA of E, because you too could be enjoying the services membership brings.

If you are thinking of joining a club, then write to the Association and find out which of its member clubs meets near you.

Apply to	Mr J.E. Gowers, at the address above
Age range	9–16
Joining fee	none
Annual fee	paid by clubs
Members	4,920
Date started	1893

English Schools' Badminton Association (ESBA)

National Badminton Centre
Bradwell Road
Loughton Lodge
Milton Keynes MK8 9LA
Tel: (0908) 568822

Is your school a member of this Association? – if so, *you* can enjoy the services it offers. Both national and regional events are organised by ESBA; they include international tournaments, national championships, regional tournaments, the highly honoured four-day ESBA/Carlton Inter-Counties Championship, and the Barclays Bank National Schools Badminton Championships for individual schools.

During the summer holidays ESBA organises three coaching courses; one is reserved for national standard players, but the other two are available to anyone. ESBA also has a scheme by which you can gain primary, bronze, silver, gold and supreme awards; this is the ESBA Carlton Award Scheme, which began in April 1983. Other attractions of ESBA include badges, stickers, ties and information packs which you can buy, together with several publications including a diary of events with dates of forthcoming tournaments.

Membership is not only for schools; you can join, individually, too.

Apply to	Administrative Secretary, at the address above
Age range	9–16
Joining fee	none
Annual fee	B individual membership
Date started	1965

Scottish Badminton Union (SBU)

Cockburn Centre
40 Bogmoor Place
Glasgow G51 4TQ
Tel: (041) 445 1218

Living in Scotland and interested in badminton? If so, the SBU is well worth joining. This is the governing body for badminton in Scotland, and accepts both clubs and individuals as members.

Each year SBU holds a Scottish Championship Tournament, Scottish National Championships, Scottish Open Championships, a circuit of Premier Open Tournaments, and Group Competitions for junior players. It also chooses Scottish international teams, and arranges international matches.

SBU runs courses for players who want to improve their game; some of these are open to anyone, others for players at advanced standards; others are for invited players in various age groups. All are held at either the Inverclyde National Sports Training Centre, or at the six-court badminton centre in Shieldhall, Glasgow.

Members can also buy the union's publications, which include guides to the game, and receive the quarterly magazine *Scottish Badminton*; this contains news, articles, and photographs, and has a special section for junior members.

Apply to	Miss Anne Smillie, at the address above
Age range	9–16
Joining fee	none
Annual fee	A
Members	11,850

Welsh Badminton Union (WBU)

Lyn-Wood
Talygarn
Pontyclun
Mid- Glamorgan CF7 9BZ
Tel: (0443) 225427

Just as England and Scotland have official bodies representing badminton in their countries so does Wales — the Welsh Badminton Union. If you live in Wales and either want to play badminton, or already do so, how about joining? Both clubs and individuals can join and enjoy the meetings, the National Championships, South and North Wales Championships, and a national squad coaching programme leading to international competitions.

The Union can provide information on the game, and publishes a handbook, annual report and a magazine, *Badminton in Wales*, three or four times a year. It can also tell you where your nearest club meets.

Apply to	Mrs Maureen Hybart, at the address above
Age range	9–16
Joining fee	further information on request
Annual fee	as above
Members	5,168
Date started	1928

British Baseball Federation

East Park Lido
Hull
N Humberside HU8 9AW

Baseball is played worldwide, but the history of the game has many links with Great Britain. The first recognised games were played in America in Hoboken, New Jersey, in 1845 between the New York Knickerbockers and the New York Nine, and the British Baseball Federation was founded a little later, in 1890. In recent years baseball has become a major attraction on television and is now an Olympic sport.

Softball is a variation of the sport and it too is enjoying worldwide interest. In Europe softball has been played more by ladies than men, but now male teams and mixed teams are fostering interest throughout the world.

The BBF has a development programme covering all aspects of the sport's progress and youth figures very prominently in these plans. Children up to the age of 10yrs can play 'T' Ball, a game based on baseball rules but where the batter hits from a tee — an advantage of this game is that it can be played indoors. Under the BBF Youth programme boys and girls up to the age of 16 play to official rules but with some slight changes in the playing area and more stringent safety rules on stealing bases.

To play baseball and enjoy the sport requires coaching in throwing and catching the ball, and coordination between eye and hands to enable you to hit the ball when the pitcher throws.

Clubs are in existence throughout the UK and have qualified coaches. Youth leagues operate within the regions and winners of these leagues play-off each year to capture the title 'British Youth Champions'. A chance to represent Great Britain in international competition is offered by selection to the Great Britain Under 18yrs team.

Apply to	the address above
Age range	9–16
Joining fee	D for a club, including insurance
Annual fee	none for juniors
Date started	1890

Welsh Baseball Union (WBU)

46 Hoel Nant Castan
Rhiwbina
Cardiff
Tel: (0222) 627343

If you live in Wales and want to play baseball then the Welsh Baseball Union offers you a chance to take part in league competitions, and to compete for the Youth Challenge Cup. Also, each year, the union honours the Most Promising Player for the year, who can be chosen from the junior members. The WBU aims to promote and foster the game of baseball and to encourage social activities amongst its members. Baseball clubs and societies can join, and if you want advice on starting this sport the union will be pleased to help.

Apply to	Mr W.J. Freeman, Secretary, at the address above
Age range	9–16
Joining fee	none
Annual fee	paid by clubs
Members	5 leagues, 70 clubs and schools
Date started	1905

THE BASEBALL FIELD

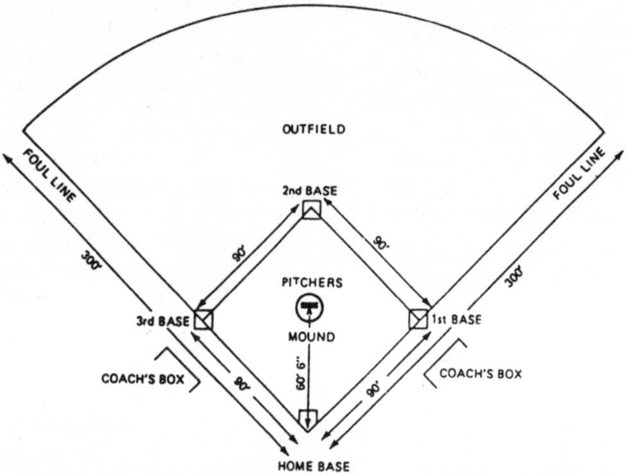

English Basketball Association (EBBA)

Calomax House
Lupton Avenue
Leeds LS9 7EE
Tel: (0532) 496044

Basketball was introduced by the American James Naismith in 1891. It is a fast-moving game usually played indoors. During this century, especially since the Second World War (1939-45), basketball has grown into a major sport, and is now represented in the Olympic Games.

EBBA promotes basketball through meetings, coaching, exhibitions, competitions, study groups, and information. It also runs visits and outings. As a member you can benefit from all of these, perhaps even qualifying for the Junior Championships, and receiving *Basketball Monthly* with articles and news about the game. EBBA also runs a Player Proficiency Award Scheme, which tests your basic skills in basketball — shooting, passing and dribbling. The tests for these awards are conducted by club coaches, youth leaders and teachers; those who pass win a cloth badge and certificate. There are Mini Basketball Awards open to children under thirteen years of age, so everyone can take part.

Apply to	Mr Paul Lawrence, at the address above
Age range	9–16
Joining fee	none
Annual fee	A
Members	16,900 including clubs
Date started	1936

Irish Basketball Association Limited (IBBA LTD)

53 Middle Abbey Street
Dublin 1
Tel: (01) 733817 or (01) 733476

If you are interested in playing basketball and live in Ireland you should think about joining this Association. Irish basketball is probably Ireland's fastest growing sport. As a member of IBBA you can take part in national and regional tournaments, and maybe even get into an international team. IBBA publishes a diary/yearbook which gives details of national league fixtures. There is also a magazine, *Basketball Ireland*, which is sent to members.

Connected to IBBA are three associations especially for school children. The Irish Minisport movement for primary schools has a membership of over 20,000; it organises a national festival, and coaching courses for over 200 children at the McDonalds Coaching Clinics and Exhibition Game. Two full days of coaching are given, followed a week later by an exhibition game, attended by over 1,200 Mini Basketball players. The AOS caters for secondary girls' schools; school teams compete in an All-Ireland Championship, and in inter-regional tournaments, as well as provide members for the international teams. IBBA, for boys' secondary schools, runs inter-provincial competitions and members can take part in national and international competitions.

Apply to	Louise Wall, at the address above
Age range	9–16
Joining fee	none
Annual fee	free
Members	7,947 plus school and college clubs
Date started	1945

Scottish Basketball Association (SBA)

8 Frederick Street
Edinburgh EH2 2HB
Tel: (031) 225 7143

The SBA promotes and controls basketball in Scotland. When you join you can take part in SBA competitions, and ask for information about basketball from the Association's staff.

Apply to	Ms Elizabeth Dudgeon, Secretary, at the address above
Age range	further information on request
Joining fee	as above
Annual fee	as above
Members	2,130
Date started	1947

Scottish Schools' Basketball Association (SSBA)

c/o Scottish Basketball Association
8 Frederick Street
Edinburgh EH2 2HB
Tel: (031) 225 7143

This Association encourages the playing of basketball in Scottish schools. If you play basketball at school you could take part in competitions organised by the SSBA, and receive a free monthly newsletter keeping you up-to-date with your sport.

Apply to	Mr Gordon Blair, Secretary, at the address above
Age range	further information on request
Joining fee	as above
Annual fee	as above
Members	as above
Date started	1962

Billiards and Snooker Control Council (B & SCC)

Coronet House
Queen Street
Leeds LS1 2TN
Tel: (0532) 440586

The game of billiards can be traced back in history to the sixth century BC. Today it continues to grow in popularity worldwide. Billiards is particularly popular in North America, England, Sweden, France, and Japan. In Japan during the early 1960s, 9,000 new billiard halls were opened in one year!

The B & SCC is the controlling body for games played in the United Kingdom, and it organises national competitions for non-professional players. It also publishes official rules for the game, and a newsletter, which members receive twice a year. The Council is very keen for more young people to take up this challenging sport, and welcomes requests for more information and new members.

Apply to	the Secretary, at the address above
Age range	9–16
Joining fee	none
Annual fee	A
Members	4,863
Date started	1885

British Crown Green Bowling Association (BCGBA)

14 Leighton Avenue
Maghull
Liverpool L31 0AH
Tel: (051) 526 8367

If you want to know more about the game of crown green bowls, and whether a club meets near you, write to this Association which will be pleased to help you. If you decide to join the BCGBA, you will receive its official handbook once a year, and be able to take part in its competitions.

Apply to	Mr R. Holt, Honorary Secretary, at the address above
Age range	further information on request
Joining fee	paid for by clubs
Annual fee	as above
Members	about 130,000
Date started	1910

Scottish Women's Indoor Bowling Association

1 Underwood Road
Burnside
Rutherglen
Glasgow GY3 3TE
Tel: (041) 647 5810

If you are a girl living in Scotland, and like the idea of indoor bowls for a hobby, then this is the Association for you. Find out more by writing now.

Apply to	Mrs R. Thompson, Honorary Secretary, at address above
Age range	further information on request
Joining fee	as above
Annual fee	as above

English Bowling Association (EBA)

Lyndhurst Road
Worthing
W Sussex BN11 2AZ
Tel: (0903) 820222

The flat-green game of bowling used to be thought of as a sport for senior citizens, but today more and more young people are taking part and finding out what fun this very competitive game can be. The EBA promotes flat-green bowling in England, so if you want to know more about the game and your local clubs, just write and ask for information.

Apply to	the Secretary at the address above
Age range	further information on request
Joining fee	as above
Annual fee	as above
Members	as above
Date started	1903

Amateur Boxing Association of England (ABA)

Francis House
Francis Street
London SW1P 1DE
Tel: (01) 828 8571

You can join the ABA as an individual, through a boxing club, or through your school. If you are thinking of taking up boxing, the ABA will provide you with information about the sport and where and when your nearest member club meets. Once you have joined a club you will be able to take part in competitions put on by the ABA; you may even become good enough to take part in its annual championships and international tournaments.

Apply to	Mr Clive Howe, Secretary, at the address above
Age range	11–16
Joining fee	paid for by your club or school
Annual fee	as above
Members	about 31,000
Date started	1880

Welsh Amateur Boxing Association (WABA)

8 Erw Wen
Rhiwbina
Cardiff CF4 6JW
Tel: (0222) 623566

WABA promotes and controls amateur boxing in Wales, and organises competitions for members. If you live in Wales and are thinking of taking up boxing as a sport just write to the WABA, who will be pleased to send you full information.

Apply to	Mr J.K. Watkins at the address above
Age range	9–16
Joining fee	paid for by clubs
Annual fee	as above
Members	92 clubs
Date started	1910

Association of Cricket Statisticians (ACS)

Haughton Mill
Retford
Nottinghamshire
Tel: (0623) 860145

Cricket has been played under recognised rules at least since the beginning of the eighteenth century, the first definite match on record being held in 1697.

The ACS aims to bring together all those whose hobby is cricket records so that their work can be co-ordinated and the best published so that all members can benefit. Copies of these publications are free to members, or sold at a special low price if more specialised. Four times a year members receive *The Cricket Statistician*, a lively magazine with articles written by members. Other publications include a series of County and State booklets, and a series of books containing the full scores of every first-class match both home and overseas. With Newnes, the publisher, the Association also publishes *Who's Who in Cricket,* containing biographies of every cricketer to appear in first-class matches in the British Isles, and based on members' own research. The ACS also publishes Minor Counties Annuals and Second XI Annuals, with brief biographies of current players, full averages, potted scores and records.

Each spring a major meeting is held, at which all members are welcome. The Association also has 'specialists' in most branches of cricket statistics, who will be pleased to help or advise you.

Apply to	the address above
Age range	older readers
Joining fee	none
Annual fee	B
Members	1,200
Date started	1973

The Cricket Society

50 Westbrook
Lustrells Vale
Saltdean
East Sussex BN2 8FZ
Tel: (0273) 32784

If you love cricket then this is the Society for you. As a member you can attend meetings in London, Bath and Birmingham to see films, and to listen to talks by famous cricketers and other well-known personalities from the cricketing world. Twice a year you will receive *The Journal*, and eight times a year the Society's newsletter *The News Bulletin*.

Each year the Cricket Society presents a number of awards and prizes to cricketers and cricket writers. These include the Wetherall Awards for the leading all-rounders in English first-class cricket, Schools' cricket and Repton School, the Most Promising Young Cricketer Award, the A.A. Thomson Fielding Prize for the best schoolboy fieldsman, the Sir John Hobbs Silver Jubilee Memorial Prize for the outstanding English schoolboy player under 16, and the Annual Coaching Scholarships presented to four promising boys aged between 11 and 17 years.

Apply to	Mr E.C. Rice, Honorary General Secretary, at the address above
Age range	9–16
Joining fee	none
Annual fee	C
Members	over 2,000
Date started	1945

Women's Cricket Association (WCA)

16 Upper Woburn Place
London WC1H 0QP
Tel: (01) 387 3423

Women's cricket was played in England as long ago as the eighteenth century, and now flourishes in the twentieth century, especially in India where it is very popular. Mixed cricket is being introduced in primary schools and in the early years of secondary schools. For girls, who are both enthusiastic and good players, membership of a club or school which belongs to this Association means that they could play cricket for area and national teams.

Individuals can also join and will receive a Year Book, a regular *News Bulletin* and an annual Fixture Card, which keep them fully informed about activities and matches. The WCA also organises coaching all year round at indoor and outdoor nets, and special courses catering for all levels of ability from beginners to national team members. Once a year a coaching week, open to all players, provides for individual coaching in pleasant surroundings in a holiday atmosphere. Join now and you could be enjoying the opportunities the WCA provides.

Apply to	Mrs C.A. Duley, at the address above
Age range	9–16
Joining fee	none
Annual fee	none
Members	308
Date started	1926

Croquet Association

The Hurlingham Club
Ranelagh Gardens
London SW6 3PR
Tel: (01) 736 3148

It is thought that croquet was developed from a game played in France as long ago as the thirteenth century. By the 1850s it had become one of the most popular outdoor sports in England. Today it is not as popular, but even so it is an enjoyable garden game, which can be played by all the family.

Whether you enjoy a game of garden croquet, or want to compete in the growing sport of Association Croquet, the Croquet Association has something to offer you. Six times a year you receive *Croquet*, an attractively produced magazine, which as well as reporting on tournaments and local club and federation news, also provides personality profiles and coaching advice. Every February a complete guide to the next season's tournaments and how to enter them is sent to all members. You can buy a wide range of publications on the game at lower prices, and attend courses and seminars to learn how to improve your game. You also get a proper handicap, even if you do not play in tournaments, and this is valid for inter-club friendlies, internal tournaments and every other occasion. If you do want to compete in competitions the Association organises a National Junior Tournament and an Inter-Schools Team Event.

Apply to	Mr B.C. Macmillan, Secretary, at the address above
Age range	9–16
Joining fee	none
Annual fee	C
Members	2,600
Date started	1896

Cyclists' Touring Club (CTC)

Cotterell House
69 Meadrow
Godalming
Surrey GU7 3HS
Tel: (04868) 7217

Cycling as a sport is over one hundred years old, and hundreds of thousands of people are members of touring clubs, particularly in France, Belgium, Italy, England and the United States of America. Cycling as a hobby or sport is fun, healthy and economical, and in a town it can be the quickest and easiest way to get around, as eight million regular riders in Britain have discovered. Whether you use a bike for leisure or for everyday riding about town, the Cyclists' Touring Club is well worth joining.

Accidents do happen whilst cycling, but if you were not to blame, membership of the Club provides you with the free services of a professional legal aid staff and solicitors, who will work to get you full compensation. If you were to blame, public liability or third party insurance worth up to £500,000 covers you for any claim made against you while cycling.

Unfortunately there is an increasing number of bike thefts — an estimated £10 million worth of cycles are stolen each year — and the CTC cycle insurance policy, available only to members, offers you a guaranteed payment up to the insured value of your bike, with no reduction for wear and tear.

The CTC campaigns on behalf of all cyclists. Its concerns include higher standards of road maintenance, cycle access to the countryside and protecting the rural environment, and better facilities for bikes on trains.

The Club's magazine *Cycletouring* comes to members six times a year, with a wealth of information on all aspects of cycling. The CTC annual handbook which has five thousand addresses for accommodation and repairers, and touring and general cycling information, is also free to members.

Apply to	the address above
Age range	9–16
Joining fee	none
Annual fee	C
Members	25,000
Date started	1878

Road Time Trials Council (RTTC)

Dallacre House
Mill Road
Yarwell
Peterborough PE8 6PS
Tel: (0780) 782464

To take part in road time trials you need a modern lightweight bicycle with the mudguards and saddle bag removed, and to be a member of an officially recognised club. If you want to know which is your local club write to the RTTC for the address.

Once a member, the Council's handbook will inform you each year when and where time trial events will take place — there are just over two thousand of such events all over the United Kingdom. The handbook, published in January, also contains all the rules of the sport, the winners of the National Championships and fascinating tables showing how records at various distances are getting faster and faster.

The National Championships include a National Junior 25-Mile Championship, entry to which is through area heats and finals. You will find that there are also a number of juvenile events specially for twelve to sixteen year olds.

During the winter clubs arrange indoor training sessions, and it is also a time for club dinners and for presenting prizes. At a national dinner, prize presentation and dance, the National Time Trial Champions of the year receive their awards, including the Junior Best All-Rounder, which goes to the rider who records the best average speed for ten and twenty-five miles.

Apply to Mr Dudley Roberts, National Secretary, at the address above
Age range 12–16
Joining fee none
Annual fee paid by your club
Members 760 clubs
Date started 1922

British Darts Organisation Limited (BDO)

2 Pages Lane
Muswell Hill
London N10 1PS
Tel: (01) 883 5544/5

If you enjoy playing darts, or are thinking of starting to play, this organisation can provide you with information, especially about the meetings and competitions it organises.

Apply to the address above
Age range further information on request
Joining fee as above
Annual fee as above
Members 30,000
Date started 1973

Scottish Darts Organisation (SDA)

3 St Fillans Grove
Aberdour
Burntisland
Fife KY3 0XG
Tel: (0383) 860546

Interested in darts and living in Scotland? If so, this is your Association which organises competitions and exhibitions, and provides its members with information, and a newsletter six times a year.

Apply to the address above
Age range further information on request
Joining fee as above
Annual fee as above
Members 36,372 and 16 area organisations
Date started 1971

British Drag Racing Association (BDRA)

'Bakersfield'
29 West Drive
Caldecote
Cambridgeshire CB3 7NY
Tel: (0954) 210028

This Association promotes drag racing of cars and motorcycles, and will be pleased to provide you with information about this exciting sport.

Apply to	Mrs Yvonne Tramm, General Secretary, at the address above
Age range	9–16
Joining fee	D for 16 year olds and families
Annual fee	C for 9–15
Members	about 1,000
Date started	1964

Amateur Fencing Association (AFA)

The De Beaumont Centre
83 Perham Road
London W14 9SP
Tel: (01) 385 7442

Every fencer in the United Kingdom, whatever his or her standard, can benefit from the services offered by this Association.

When you join AFA you are covered by a worldwide insurance scheme which covers you while fencing, and travelling to and from fencing. You receive information about fencing competitions, and three times a year the magazine *Sword*. Competitions which you can enter include county, section, NAGC under-fourteens and under-sixteens, novices, the Winton Cup, open, and the national under-twenties. You can also take part in all AFA courses and awards.

Apply to	the Secretary, at the address above
Age range	9–16
Joining fee	none
Annual fee	B
Members	3,981
Date started	1902

British Field Sports' Society (BFSS)

59 Kennington Road
London SE1 7PZ
Tel: (01) 928 4742

If you hunt, shoot, fish, go coursing or fly falcons you should think about belonging to this Society. The BFSS aims to safeguard your sport by presenting the arguments in favour of field sports, and working for the conservation of the countryside to free it from chemical pollution, from the destruction of hedgerows, woods, copses and wetlands, and from poaching, illegal trapping, poisoning and vandalism.

To encourage country sports clubs in schools the BFSS has formed a Students' Country Sports Campaign which provides information, advice and practical help, sends out a free termly newsletter, promotes meetings for members to hear guest speakers and see videos and sports quizzes, and organises local events such as visits to kennels, gun safety demonstrations and coaching.

Apply to	the Membership Dept, at the address above
Age range	older readers
Joining fee	none
Annual fee	B
Members	60,500
Date started	1930

Anglers' Cooperative Association (ACA)

Midland Bank Chambers
Westgate
Grantham
Lincolnshire NG31 6LE
Tel: (0476) 61008

Over three million people regularly go fishing in Great Britain. The ACA campaigns against the pollution of water so that these fishermen and women can enjoy their sport. If you enjoy fishing and want to see our rivers and streams free from pollution then support the ACA.

When you join this Association you will receive the *ACA Review* once a year, and have the opportunity to compete for the British Pike Angling Championship.

Apply to	Mr Allen Edwards, at the address above
Age range	9–16
Joining fee	none
Annual fee	A
Members	9,120
Date started	1948

National Federation of Anglers (NFA)

2 Wilson Street
Derby DE1 1PG
Tel: (0332) 362000

The NFA is concerned with improving freshwater fishery laws, combating river pollution, and the development of common fishing waters. If you join this Federation you can ask it for advice and information, and also take part in competitions.

Apply to	the address above
Age range	further information on request
Joining fee	as above
Annual fee	as above
Members	500,400
Date started	1903

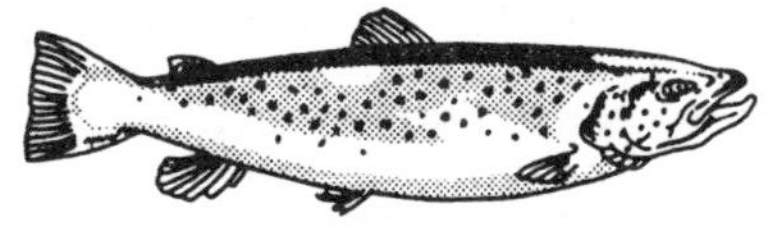

Scottish Anglers' National Association (SANA)

307 West George Street
Glasgow G2 4LB
Tel: (041) 221 7206

This is the governing body for trout fly-fishing and angling in Scotland, and it organises national and international angling matches. If you would like to take part write to SANA and ask for information.

Apply to	the address above
Age range	further information on request
Joining fee	as above
Annual fee	as above
Members	as above
Date started	1880

Scottish Federation of Sea Anglers (SFSA)

18 Ainslie Place
Edinburgh EH3 6AU
Tel: (031) 225 7611

If you live in Scotland and want to know more about sea fishing either from the shore or in boats, then the SFSA can help you. When you have joined the SFSA you can take part in coaching courses and you will receive a quarterly newsletter. Each year *The Festival Guide and Handbook* provides you with useful information about the tides, details about future events and competitions, for instance the Junior (Open) Boat Championships, and lists of member clubs including junior clubs. Individual boat and shore championships are held each year, for which trophies are presented. The SFSA is also active in the conservation of species of fish under threat.

Apply to	The Secretary, at the address above
Age range	9–16
Joining fee	none
Annual fee	B
Members	306
Date started	1961

The Air League

4, Hamilton Place
London W1V 0BQ
Tel: (01) 499 6400

If you are interested in any aspect of flying, the Air League is the Association for you. Since it began the League has done much to help British aviation. It started the Air Defence Cadet Corps, which became the ATC. It also began Empire Air Days, one of the forerunners of today's major air displays. It has been involved in successful campaigns to provide more modern fixed-wing aircraft for the Queen's flight, to support the vertical/short take off and landing concept for military aircraft, to reduce tax on fuel, and to press for government funding of the Airbus A320 project.

Young people who wish to learn to fly, either as a hobby or as a preparation for a career in aviation, are encouraged to compete for flying scholarships which are provided by the Air League Educational Trust.

When you join the Air League you receive a monthly magazine *Air Pictorial*, and the Air League newsletters, together with occasional reports and notices, and invitations to lectures, receptions and other events. Junior members can have reduced entrance fees for certain air shows.

Apply to	the Secretary-General, at the address above
Age range	older readers
Joining fee	none
Annual fee	B
Members	764
Date started	1909

British Gliding Association (BGA)

Kimberley House
Vaughan Way
Leicester
Tel: (0533) 531051

Flying in modern gliders means that you can explore the skies for the whole day long, travelling perhaps two or three hundred miles before you return home. It is not difficult to become a safe glider pilot. As long as you are reasonably fit you can learn to glide from sixteen years of age. Once you have trained you can either fly cross-country or enter gliding competitions.

If you wish to take up gliding write to the BGA which will tell you about holiday gliding courses and gliding clubs in Britain. The BGA can tell you about books on gliding, and answer any questions about this exciting sport.

Apply to	the address above
Age range	16
Joining fee	none
Annual fee	paid by clubs
Members	further information on request
Date started	as above

Scottish Gliding Union (SGU)

Portmoak Airfield
Scotlandwell
Kinross
Tayside KY13 7JJ
Tel: (059 284) 543

You can enjoy gliding with the SGU at Portmoak Airfield whether you live in Scotland or not. The Union organises residential courses, and offers instruction in single and two-seater gliders. Holiday gliding courses, intended for beginners, are available from April to September. You may just want to experience the excitement of gliding over the beautiful countryside around Loch Leven. Flights are available for a modest cost, and visitors are always welcome at the airfield.

Apply to	the Secretary at the address above
Age range	16
Joining fee	further information on request
Annual fee	as above
Members	as above
Date started	1934

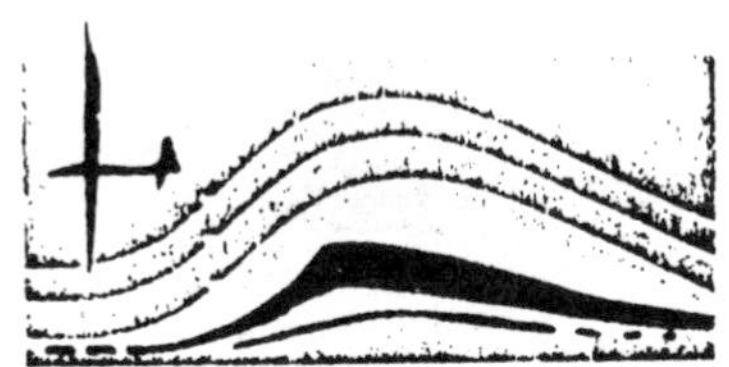

Association of Football Statisticians (AFS)

22 Bretons
Basildon
Essex SS15 5BY
Tel: (0268) 416020

Your hobby may not only include watching football matches but also collecting facts and figures about the game and its players. If so, this Association can help you. It provides a wide range of publications—over ninety titles—not available elsewhere, a magazine every two months, contact with others sharing your hobby through a list of members, the use of a library with two thousand books and magazines on football, an information service, and occasional meetings throughout the United Kingdom.

Apply to	Mr Ray Spiller, at the address above
Age range	older readers
Joining fee	none
Annual fee	C
Members	1,090
Date started	1978

English Schools' Football Association (ESFA)

4A Eastgate Street
Stafford ST16 2NQ
Tel: (0785) 51142

If you are a member of a school football team, that team can join this Association and compete for the Gillette Trophy, British Home Stores Trophy, Nabisco Brands Trophy, the Barclays Bank Competition, the under-19 Inter-County Championship, or Smiths Foods 6-a-side Competition. As a team member you could enter the Super Skills Award Scheme, which requires you to pass seven single tests of skill, which include touch, heading, passing, controlling and trapping, dribbling, kicking and accuracy of shooting. There are different awards for different levels of achievement, as you improve you move from one level to another.

As a member of ESFA your school team will receive a handbook each year, and a newsletter three times a year.

Apply to	the address above
Age range	9–16
Joining fee	none
Annual fee	paid by school
Members	14,000 schools
Date started	1904

Scottish Amateur Football Association (SAFA)

'Beechwood'
Gateside Road
Barrhead
Glasgow G78 1EP

Living in Scotland and interested in playing amateur football? If the club you play for is a member of SAFA you will be able to take part in competitions.

Not a member of a club but wanting to join one? Then write to SAFA for the address of your nearest club.

Apply to	Mr Iain McTweed, at the address above
Age range	9–16
Joining fee	none
Annual fee	your club pays
Members	72,900
Date started	1909

Scottish Schools' Football Association (SSFA)

5 Forth Park Gardens
Kirkcaldy
Fife KY2 5TD
Tel: (0592) 261811

If you live in Scotland and your school is a member of SSFA, your football team can join in inter-school competitions. As a member of the team you may even be chosen to play in an international match organised by SSFA.

About three times a year your school will receive a newsletter from the Association, and a handbook will be sent each year, giving information about future events.

Apply to	Mr R.M. Docherty, General Secretary, at the address above
Age range	9–16
Joining fee	none
Annual fee	your school pays
Members	1,550
Date started	1904

Womens' Football Association Limited (WFA)

11 Portsea Mews
Portsea Place
London W2 2BN
Tel: (01) 402 9388

If you are a girl and want to play football this Association can tell you where your nearest club meets. The WFA also organises competitions for you to take part in once you are a member of a club.

Apply to	the address above
Age range	further information on request
Joining fee	as above
Annual fee	as above
Members	6,243
Date started	1969

Scottish Ladies' Golfing Association (SLGA)

5 Brownhills House
St Andrews
Fife KY16 8PL

If you are a girl and belong to a golf club in Scotland, you can join the SLGA, and take part in the Girls' Close Golf Championship and the Girls' Open Stroke Play Championship.

Apply to	through your golf club
Age range	11–16
Joining fee	none
Annual fee	A
Members	33,300
Date started	1904

British Amateur Gymnastics' Association (BAGA)

2 Buckingham Avenue East
Slough
Berkshire SL1 3EA
Tel: (0753) 32763

You have to join a gymnastic club to belong to this Association, which offers awards for proficiency in all sections of gymnastics — the Coca-Cola BAGA Awards, the Midland Bank Sports Aerobatics Awards, the Lilia-White Modern Rhythmic Gymnastics Awards, the Gold Top Milk Awards for Women and Girls, and the Philishave Gymnastics Awards for Men and Boys. In addition you will receive the magazine, *Gymnast*, six times a year, and *Junior Gymnast*, twice a year. Write for the address of your Regional Secretary and nearest club.

Apply to	the Membership Secretary, at the above address
Age range	9–16
Joining fee	none
Annual fee	varies with club
Members	70,000
Date started	1888

Scottish Amateur Gymnastics' Association (SAGA)

18 Ainslie Place
Edinburgh EH3 6AU
Tel: (031) 226 4401

If you live in Scotland and enjoy gymnastics at school or a club, you could be taking part in competitions, and getting a newsletter ten times a year.

Apply to	Mrs Pam Scott, at the address above
Age range	9–16
Joining fee	paid by school or club
Annual fee	as above
Members	185
Date started	1890

British Handball Association

Handball House,
32 Grove Place
Bedford MK40 3JJ
Tel: (0234) 213597

Handball has been played in this country for over twenty years. Games like handball were played by the ancient Greeks and Romans as far back as 600 BC, and during the Middle Ages in France and England. In the United Kingdom this skilful, highly competitive ball game is becoming very popular. Junior teams take part in national and regional leagues, as well as knock-out tournaments. If you are nine years old you play mini-handball, if ten to fourteen years old, junior handball, and if over fourteen years handball, the Olympic sport for both men and women.

If you would like your school to take part in this exciting and fast sport, ask a teacher to write for more information. When your school is a member you may even qualify for the national training squads for Under-14 and Under-16 teams, and be able to take part in regional coaching programmes.

Apply to	the General Secretary, at the address above
Age range	9–16
Joining fee	paid for by schools
Annual fee	paid for by schools
Date started	1968

All England Women's Hockey Association (AEWHA)

Third Floor
Argyle House
29-31 Euston Road
London NW1 2SD
Tel: (01) 278 6340

Does your school have a girls' hockey team? If so, it can join this Association and your team will be able to take part in national championships for schools in both outdoor and indoor hockey. You may find yourself playing for your country, or even for the England Under-18 team!

For those of you who are over fifteen years old, there is a residential coaching course held each year, as well as regional courses. The AEWHA publishes a handbook and other helpful publications including *The Hockey Field Magazine*.

Apply to	the address above
Age range	9–16
Joining fee	paid by school
Annual fee	paid by school
Members	3,780
Date started	1895

The Hockey Association (HA)

16 Upper Woburn Place
London WC1H 0QD
Tel: (01) 387 9315

Schools and hockey clubs can join this Association, which is the governing body for all male players of outdoor and indoor hockey. If you play hockey for a school or club which is a member of the HA, you can take part in coaching schemes and your team is able to take part in competitions. You may even find yourself chosen to play in international teams!

Six times a year the HA sends its members the *Hockey Digest* and, once a year, a handbook, which keep you up-to-date with your hobby.

If you want to know if a club, which is a member of this Association, meets near you then write to the HA.

Apply to	Miss Debbie Smith or Mrs Kim Hall, at the address above
Age range	9–16
Joining fee	none
Annual fee	depends on school or club
Members	39,622
Date started	1886

National Roller Hockey Association of Great Britain (NRHA)

528 Loose Road
Maidstone
Kent ME15 9UF
Tel: (0622) 43155

This is the governing body of roller hockey, so if you are wanting to join a roller hockey club write to NRHA and it will tell you who to contact in your area. Once you are a member you will be able to train and eventually take part in competitions organised by the NRHA.

Apply to	the address above
Age range	9–16
Joining fee	paid for by clubs
Annual fee	B associate membership
Members	1,565
Date started	1912

Scottish Hockey Association (SHA)

18 Ainslie Place
Edinburgh EH3 6AU
Tel: (031) 226 4401

This Association promotes men's hockey in Scotland, and includes three thousand schoolboys in its membership. If you would like to know more, and to take part in the competitions organised by SHA, write and ask for information.

Apply to	the address above
Age range	further information on request
Joining fee	as above
Annual fee	as above
Members	6,075
Date started	1901

Welsh Hockey Association (WHA)

(Cymdeithas Hoci Cymru)
40 Purcell Road
Penarth
South Glamorgan CF6 2QN
Tel: (0222) 708475

This Association promotes men's hockey in Wales, and organises training and competitions. If you would like to know more about WHA, or where your nearest club meets, then write and the Association will be pleased to help.

Apply to	Mr D.C. Pedwell, Youth Chairman, at the address above
Age range	further information on request
Joining fee	as above
Annual fee	as above
Members	120
Date started	1895

Welsh Women's Hockey Association (WSSA)

5 Clayton Court
Mold
Clwyd CH7 1TW
Tel: (0352) 3004

This Association organises training and competitions for women's hockey in Wales. Interested in knowing more? Then write and ask for information

Apply to	Mrs A. Humphreys, at the address above
Age range	depends on individual clubs
Joining fee	A
Annual fee	depends on individual clubs
Members	2,000
Date started	1898

All England Women's Lacrosse Association (AEWLA)

16 Upper Woburn Place
London WC14 0QJ
Tel: (01) 387 4430

The modern game of lacrosse developed from the game baggataway played by North American Indians. They played the game between goals as much as three miles apart with as many as five hundred players, and used it as a bravery test for young men, and as a means of settling inter-tribal arguments. It first came to England in 1867, with a series of demonstrations by a party of Indians. Since that time lacrosse has been developed in schools and clubs, and is now a well-established sport. Recently pop-lacrosse has been developed to help make the game even more popular. It is an exciting game which can be quickly learnt, and is full of fun.

When you join the AEWLA you will receive information about how to play lacrosse and the sort of equipment to buy, and a quarterly magazine *Lacrosse*, full of news, letters and reports. The Association also offers coaching and a range of publications.

If you belong to a school team, then your school can join the AEWLA. However, if you would like to play lacrosse, but do not know where your nearest club meets, then write and ask the AEWLA.

Apply to	Mrs J.O'Neill, Development Officer, at the address above
Age range	9–16
Joining fee	none
Annual fee	B
Members	1,010
Date started	1912

All Wales Ladies' Lacrosse Association (AWLLA)

3 Tyla Teg
Pantmawr
Whitchurch
Cardiff CF4 6XL

If you are a girl living in Wales and wanting to play lacrosse the AWLLA will be able to tell you about the game, and give you the name of the club playing nearest to your home.

Apply to	Mrs W.A. Williams, Honorary Secretary at the address above
Age range	further information on request
Joining fee	as above
Annual fee	as above
Members	as above
Date started	1924

English Lacrosse Union (ELU)

70 High Road
Rayleigh
Essex SS6 7AD
Tel: (0268) 770758 evenings and weekends

The ELU is responsible for promoting the game of lacrosse in England. It organises exhibitions, competitions, and coaching, as well as providing an information service.

If you want to know more about this game and where you can join a team write to the ELU, which will be pleased to help you.

Apply to	the National Development Officer, at the address above
Age range	further information on request
Joining fee	as above
Annual fee	as above
Members	3 Lacrosse Associations

Amateur Ju-Jitsu Association (AJJA)

120 Cromer Street
London WC1H 8BS
Tel: (01) 837 4406

Wanting to take up ju-jitsu? The AJJA can tell you where your nearest club meets.

Apply to	the Honorary Secretary
Age range	further information on request
Joining fee	as above
Annual fee	as above
Members	82 clubs

Amateur Karate Association (AKA)

120 Cromer Street
London WC1H 8BS
Tel: (01) 837 4406

Interested in karate? Then this Association will be able to tell you where your nearest club meets.

Apply to	Honorary Secretary, at the address above
Age range	further information on request
Joining fee	as above
Annual fee	as above
Members	600 clubs

Amateur Kung Fu Association (AKFA)

120 Cromer Street
London WC1H 8BS
Tel: (01) 837 4406

If you are thinking of taking up kung fu, then this Association will be able to put you in touch with your local club.

Apply to	the Honorary Secretary at the address above
Age range	further information on request
Joining fee	as above
Annual fee	as above
Members	140 clubs

Martial Arts Commission

1st Floor Broadway House
15/16 Deptford Broadway
London SE8 4PE
Tel: (01) 691 3433

Martial arts including aikido, full contact, hapkido, ju-jitsu, karate, kendo, kobundo, kung fu, kyudo, shorinji kempo, tang soo do, tae kwon do, and Thai boxing. These can be learnt by sport, self-defence or meditation, but it must be remembered that martial arts are based upon methods of injuring, maiming or killing human beings. So it is very important that you learn your skills from good teachers with high reputations in their sport. The Martial Arts Commission issues a licence to such people and is able to recommend clubs where you can learn your skills safely.

In addition to this important service, the Commission also publishes useful and informative publications including *The Official Martial Arts Handbook*, which covers over twenty arts, helping beginners to know which to choose, and it includes a comprehensive list of addresses of major martial arts organisations.

Apply to	the address above
Age range	9–16
Joining fee	paid by associations to which the clubs belong
Annual fee	as above
Members	96,080 associations
Date started	1977

Scottish Judo Federation

8 Frederick Street
Edinburgh EH2 2HB
Tel: (031) 226 3566

Judo, which means 'easy way', is a combat sport which comes from the ancient martial arts of Japan. It now has worldwide appeal and received Olympic recognition in 1964. This Federation is responsible for the development of judo in Scotland.

If you are thinking of learning judo the SJF can provide you with details of the clubs in your area. There are 180 clubs altogether in Scotland. The Federation also organises competitive events at area, regional and national level for all standards of performance. Judo players wear belts of different colours which denote different levels of achievement and the SJF holds frequent promotion examinations to encourage members to improve their sport. There are also coaching sessions and player improvement courses.

Apply to	the address above
Age range	9–16
Joining fee	none
Annual fee	B
Members	5,000
Date started	about 1972

Auto-Cycle Union Youth Division (ACU Youth Division)

Millbuck House
Corporation Street
Rugby
Warwickshire CV21 2DN
Tel: (0788) 70332

Looking after the interests of young motor cyclists and promoting the youth motorcycle sport are the two main aims of the ACU Youth Division. Through over two hundred clubs, activities are organised in moto-cross, grass track, speedway, sprinting and cycle trials. Each club organises regular events, and by joining more than one local club you can be competing every weekend if you want to. The control of youth competition is based upon an age and class structure, so that young people of the same age and ability on similar sized motorcycles are grouped together.

Before buying a machine or joining a club it is best to talk to others already competing, and visit one or two club events. Once you have joined a club and want to start competing you have to get a competition licence which is issued on a class basis. The cost of the licence is £5 per class.

If you want to know where your local clubs meet and the type of competitions they hold, write to the ACU Youth Division and it will be pleased to help.

Apply to	the Youth Division Secretary, at the address above
Age range	9–16
Joining fee	varies with the club you join
Annual fee	as above
Members	10,000
Date started	1974

National Sprint Association Limited (NSA)

51 Hale Street
Warrington
Cheshire WA2 7PH
Tel: (0925) 573093

Sprinting involves 'blasting' your machine off from a standstill, in a straight-line, over a set distance, usually a quarter of a mile but sometimes a mile or a kilometre. The object is to cover that distance in the quickest possible time and your speed at the end — terminal speed — is measured electronically and extremely accurately. The shortest elapsed time (et) in each class determines the winner of that class.

50cc up to 3,500cc bikes compete in different classes. If your bike is a road bike you enter the various road bike classes, or if your machine is built specially for sprinting, you enter the various racing classes. There are also special junior classes from age eight to fifteen. At sixteen you move to the adult classes. There are classes for three wheelers, including motorcycle and sidecar, and vintage machines. There is a thriving hill-climbing section, for those who prefer a sprint with a bend in it!

When you join the NSA you will receive a magazine which includes news, reports, and lists of events. There are many sprint strips and hill-climb courses throughout Britain, and most weekends from March to October there is a meeting. In order to take part you

must be a NSA member. You also need a helmet in good condition with an ACU gold or silver standard sticker on it, a leather suit or leather jacket and leather jeans, boots, gloves and a visor.

Apply to	Mr Roy Fisher, 66 Henconner Lane, Bramley, Leeds
Age range	9–16
Joining fee	none
Annual fee	C (riding); B (non-riding); free, if your parent is a member
Members	500
Date started	1958

Trail Riders' Fellowship (TRF)

11 Askew Drive
Spencers Wood
Reading
Berkshire
Tel: (0734) 882781

There are green roads everywhere, some five thousand miles of which may be used by the touring motorcyclist with a taste for adventure. These roads are a journey back into history — the Great Ridgeway across the Berkshire Downs, probably Britain's oldest road, the Cam Road used since the time of the Romans as a main route up the spine of the Pennines, the Hambleton Drove Road, once a royal route into Scotland, high rocky Lake District passes, leafy back roads in Wiltshire and the West Country, old military routes over the Cheviots into Scotland, drove roads through the vast forests of Mid-Wales.

The TRF is recognised as the national body of green lane riding. Through the thirty-two groups meeting in England and Wales you can have a safe and enjoyable introduction to this sport. Most members use purpose built trial bikes, which have large wheels, low gears and high ground clearance. A learner restricted 125cc can be used by light riders with success. It is very important that your bike is as quiet as is reasonably possible, and that you are licensed, insured and wear a helmet. The bike must be fully road legal.

Local groups meet to swap information on bikes, trails, riding techniques, rights of way and law. Almost every weekend there is a trail ride, and every week there are members out exploring green lanes in informal groups. Every two months members receive a magazine full of interesting articles with photographs, reports, letters and advertisements.

Join the Fellowship and enjoy the countryside, discovering 'lost' roads that have scarcely been used for a hundred years, and at the same time support the work being undertaken to keep green lanes open.

Apply to	Mr A.J.A. Rose, Membership Secretary, 29 Anderson Drive, Kettering, Northants, NN15 5DG Tel: (0536) 522274
Age range	older readers
Joining fee	none
Annual fee	C
Members	1,202
Date started	1970

All England Netball Association Limited (AENA)

Francis House
Francis Street
London SW1P 1DE
Tel: (01) 828 2176

In 1885 Dr Joles, an American, visited Madame Osterberg's PT College near Dartford, and students there were taught basketball. By 1897 the game was being played out of doors on grass, using a small ball and waste-paper baskets on broomsticks or jumping stands. Games rules were published in 1901, and the game was now called netball.

If you join a netball club which is a member of this Association you can improve your play by taking part in the Netball Shooting Badge Scheme, the Sugarability Netball Awards, and attending coaching classes. There are matches and tournaments for you to take part in, and you may even find yourself being chosen for the English team to play in international matches. Three times a year you will have the chance to read *Club News*, and four times a year the *Netball Magazine*.

Write to AENA and find out where your nearest netball club meets.

Apply to	Ms E. Nicholl, Director at the address above
Age range	9–16
Joining fee	none
Annual fee	paid by clubs
Members	34,976
Date started	1926

Northern Ireland Netball Association Limited (NINA)

28 Cranley Gardens
Bangor
County Down BT19 2EZ

Wanting to play netball and living in Northern Ireland? The NINA will be able to put you in touch with your local club.

Apply to	the address above
Age range	further information on request
Joining fee	as above
Annual fee	as above
Members	as above
Date started	1951

Scottish Netball Association (SNA)

12 Sinclair Street
Milngavie G62 8NU

If you live in Scotland and play netball and would like to join a club, this is the Association to write to for information.

Apply to	the address above
Age range	further information on request
Joining fee	as above
Annual fee	as above
Members	as above
Date started	1947

Welsh Netball Association (WNA)

12 Bouverton Court
Llantwit Major
South Glamorgan CF6 9UJ
Tel: (04465) 6143

Wanting to join a netball club and living in Wales? This Association can tell you which of its member clubs is nearest to you, so that you can join and not only enjoy your netball, but also take part in coaching courses, and inter-club tournaments arranged by the WNA. You will enjoy reading *Netball News*, which includes dates of forthcoming matches, courses and other events.

Apply to	Mrs A. Roberts, 7 Lawson Close, Wrexham, Clwyd LL12 7BA
Age range	9–16
Joining fee	none
Annual fee	depends on your club, ranges between A and B
Members	403
Date started	1945

British Orienteering Federation (BOF)

Riversdale
Dale Road North
Darley Dale
Matlock
Derbyshire DE4 2HX
Tel: (0629) 734042

Orienteering is competitive navigation on foot. With the help of a map and compass, you have to find your way as quickly as you can between given points, using your skill to choose the best route. Events are held in woods and forests and on heath and moorland. The courses can be as short as two kilometres or as long as twelve kilometres. At all events there is a choice of four or more courses, so you can choose the one that you feel you can manage.

Write to the BOF to find out where your nearest club meets. This club will keep you informed about planned events, and will teach you the basic skills of orienteering. You will also be able to make new friends, as well as enjoy an exciting sport.

Apply to	the address above
Age range	9–16
Joining fee	varies as to which club you join
Annual fee	varies as to which club you join
Members	10,500
Date started	early 1960s

British Show Jumping Association (BSJA)

British Equestrian Centre
Stoneleigh
Kenilworth
Warwickshire CV8 2LR
Tel: (0203) 552511

There are more than fifteen thousand BSJA affiliated show competitions each year. But to compete in any; at which prize money is more than £7, you must be a member of this Association and register your horse or pony with it.

When you join you will receive a copy of the BSJA Rules and Yearbook annually, and four times a year the BSJA *Quarterly News*. For an extra payment you can receive a monthly show bulletin, which gives brief details of forthcoming shows. Membership also provides you with free third party insurance for owning and riding horses, and other insurance can be obtained at very reasonable rates.

Please note that if you wish to become a member, one of your parents or guardians must also become a full, or non-jumping, member of the Association.

Apply to	Lt Cdr W.B. Jefferis, Secretary General, at the address above
Age range	9–16
Joining fee	none
Annual fee	under 16 to ride ponies only, B; 12–16 riding ponies and/or horses, C
Members	16,000
Date started	1925

The Pony Club of Great Britain

British Equestrian Centre
Stoneleigh
Kenilworth
Warwickshire CV8 2LR
Tel: (0203) 52241

This is the largest association of riders in the world, with over 360 branches in the United Kingdom alone. When you become a member you will be able to enjoy your local branch's activities including lectures, film shows, visits to kennels, stud farms or other places of interest, horse shows, hunter trials, special children's meets of hounds, summer camps, mounted expeditions and visits of teams

abroad. There are also working rallies, which usually take place during the school holidays, where instruction in either equitation, care of saddlery or management of the pony is given, and mounted games and sports are organised. Inter-branch events to encourage team work are another popular feature of the work of the Pony Club. You can also be awarded efficiency certificates, of which there are standards, and all members are expected to try for these, and to attend the working rallies.

Having your own pony is not essential, although it is desirable, and many members hire a pony from a riding school in order to take part in mounted activities.

You can join the Pony Club through your local branch, but if you do not know where this meets then write to the Pony Club and the staff there will be happy to help.

Apply to	the Secretary, at the address above
Age range	9–16
Joining fee	A
Annual fee	C
Members	105,005
Date started	1929

The Side Saddle Association (SSA)

Foxworth Farm
Stitchins Hill
Leigh Sinton
Worcestershire WR13 5DJ
Tel: (0886) 32532

Joining this Association, which encourages and promotes side saddle riding all over the world, enables you to enter side saddle championships, obtain special rosettes and trophies, and to receive a year-book and a show and fixture list. The SSA can provide you with a list of instructors, and a list of saddlers.

The United Kingdom is divided by the SSA into fifteen areas, each of which organises shows, rallies, instruction courses, and social events. Write and find out whom to contact in your local area, so that you can take part in these too.

Apply to	Mrs P.A. Bacon, at the address above
Age range	9–16
Joining fee	B
Annual fee	C
Members	1,050
Date started	1974

Western Equestrian Society (WES)

65 Wealdbridge Road
North Weald
Essex CM16 6ES
Tel: (037) 8822827

Do you have your own horse? If so, you might like to train it to become a Western horse. This does not mean that you begin to ride like movie/rodeo/TV cowboys and indians, but that you train your horse to a very high standard. The ideal horse for this training stands around 14.2 – 15.3 hands high, possesses a low, long ground action and minimum knee and hock movement, with both substance and style, having a sturdy body with short bunchy muscles tapering off into clean straight legs proportionately shorter than, for example, a thoroughbred. If your horse does not quite meet these requirements do not give up, but expect that you may be limited in what you can achieve.

This Society will help you to train your horse, by giving guidance on how to control it through leg pressure instead of through the reins, how to 'back up', and how to circle. It also provides you with information about showing your horse.

Interested? Then write now and ask for more information.

Apply to	Mrs Barbara Carder, at the address above
Age range	9–16
Joining fee	A
Annual fee	C
Members	75
Date started	1985

Western Horsemen's Association of Great Britain (WHA)

1 Oxlip Road
Witham
Essex CM8 2XY

This Association is for all who are interested in the Western style of riding. It has qualified judges and instructors, and a series of examinations for you and your horse to take in Western horsemanship.

When you join the WHA you can take part in shows, trail rides, long distance riding, instruction clinics, film shows, barbecues, and attend lectures, and film and video shows. Once a year there is a championship show, and a European championship every two years usually held in Germany.

The sort of events you will see or take part in include horses working with cows, racing around three barrels against the clock, and pole bending — weaving back and forth through a line of upright poles at top speed without knocking any of them over. You will receive a newsletter every two months. You can call upon the WHA for advice on tack, clothing and training your horse, and there are instructional weekends at reasonable fees. Lists of publications and of riding schools offering training in Western style riding are also available from WHA.

Apply to	Mrs Chris Foster, at the address above
Age range	9–16
Joining fee	A
Annual fee	B
Members	over 400
Date started	1968

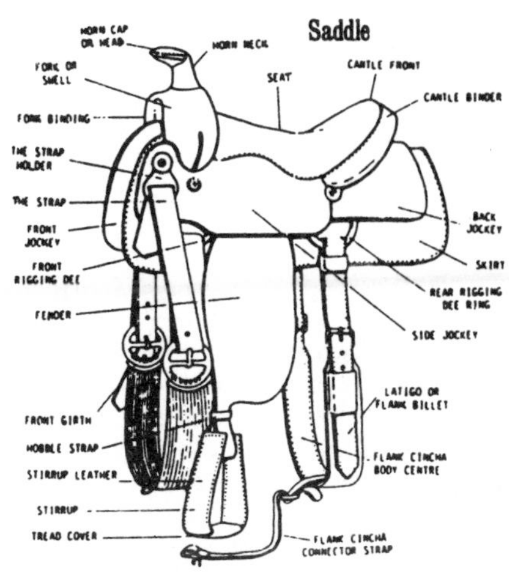

Irish Rugby Football Union (IRFU)

62 Lansdowne Road
Dublin 4
Tel: (01) 684 601

Living in Ireland and wanting to play rugby football for a club? This union has four branches — Ulster, Munster, Leinster and Connacht — each of which has an honorary secretary who will tell you about your nearest club and whom to contact.

Apply to	*Ulster:* Mr A. Holmes Secretary, Ravenhill Park, Belfast BT6 0DG *Munster:* Mr D.B. Kelly, Honorary Secretary, 'Aasleagh', 25 Castleowen, Blarney County Cork *Leinster:* Mr A.P. Squire Honorary Secretary, 99 Fairways Rathfarnham, Dublin 14 *Connacht:* Mr D.M. Crowley Honorary Secretary, Ard Ri House, Lower Abbey Gate Street Galway
Age range	9–16
Joining fee	none
Annual fee	none
Date started	1874

Rugby Football Schools' Union (RFSU)

Rugby Road
Twickenham
Middlesex TW2 7RQ
Tel: (01) 892 8161

To get the most enjoyment from playing rugby football you need to learn, practise and develop your skills. Find out if your school is a member of the RFSU, because if so you may be able to take part in the RFU Proficiency Awards and the RFSU summer courses.

There are three awards, Bronze, Silver and Gold, and you start at the Bronze and work your way up by completing seven tests – running with the ball, catching a high ball, kicking, passing the ball, kicking and catching, handling, and tackling — at one session. Your teacher in charge of games can put you through these tests.

There are summer courses for twelve to fourteen year olds who have talent, enthusiasm and ambition. During these six-day courses you can expect to improve your basic skills, learn new techniques, increase your knowledge of the game, get fitter and have the chance to gain an RFU Proficiency Award. The programmes are full of different activities, including swimming, team competitions, quizzes and videos.

If you are fifteen years old or more, and have represented your county or gained recognition at your club or school, then you can apply for another course, at which you will be coached by RFU staff and senior coaches. There is also a course for young players aged seven to twelve years of age, who attend with their fathers or mothers. This course provides a practical understanding of the basic principles of the game through demonstrations and practice of techniques. The skills covered include handling, running, kicking and contact.

Apply to	the address above
Age range	9–16
Joining fee	none
Annual fee	paid by schools
Members	2,559
Date started	1970

Rugby Football Union (RFU)

Whitton Road
Twickenham
Middlesex TW2 7RQ

Thinking of joining a rugby club? The RFU will be able to tell you which of its member clubs meets near you. Once you are a member of a club you will be able to take part with your team in competitions organised by the union. If you play rugby at school, then you too can take part in these competitions when your school becomes a member of the RFU.

Apply to	the address above
Age range	9–16
Joining fee	paid by your club or school
Annual fee	as above
Members	1,800 clubs, 2,500 schools
Date started	1871

Scottish Rugby Union (SRU)
Murrayfield
Edinburgh EH12 5PJ
Tel: (031) 337 2346

Living in Scotland and wanting to play rugby? The SRU can tell you where your nearest club meets and whom to contact. Once a member you will be able to take part in SRU competitions with your team.

Apply to	the address above
Age range	9–16
Joining fee	paid by clubs
Annual fee	paid by clubs
Members	110 clubs or unions
Date started	1973

Welsh Rugby Union (WRU)
PO Box 22
Cardiff CF1 1JL
Tel: (0222) 390111

If you live in Wales and want to play rugby this Union will be able to tell you where your nearest club meets and whom to contact. The WRU also organises competitions and coaching for you to take part in once you have joined your club.

Apply to	the address above
Age range	9–16
Joining fee	paid by your club
Annual fee	paid by your club
Members	194 clubs
Date started	1880

Rugby Fives Association Club (RFAC)
Fairbourne Lodge
Epping Green
Essex CM16 6PR
Tel: (0378) 72904

Like rugby football this game also began at Rugby, but this is where the connection between the two games ends. In fact rugby fives is more like squash, except that instead of a racquet you use a special glove with which to direct the ball. There are courts throughout the United Kingdom and when you join the RFAC you receive a pamphlet listing these, together with a welcome to call in and play whenever you are in their area.

Apply to	Mr Tom Wood, Honorary Secertary, at the address above
Age range	9–16
Joining fee	none
Annual fee	B
Members	290
Date started	1927

British Association for Shooting and Conservation (BASC)

Marford Mill
Rossett
Wrexham
Clwyd LL12 0HL
Tel: (0244) 570881

The use of shotguns and where you can use them is tightly governed by the law, but if you want to take part in this hobby, whether shooting at game or clays, this Association will be able to advise you. Such advice is only one of the services the BASC offers to you when you are a member. It also runs a wide range of courses and training schemes, and publishes codes of practice. You are covered by insurance when shooting or taking part in conservation work. The regular magazine *Shooting and Conservation* keeps you up-to-date with all aspects of your sport, and there is a mail order service offering you a wide range of books and items of interest.

By joining the BASC you can benefit from its help in developing and enjoying your sport safely, and at the same time support the Association's work in fostering a practical interest in the countryside, wildlife management and conservation.

Apply to	Mr Colin Barwell or Mr Tom Cave at the address above
Age range	9–16
Joining fee	none
Annual fee	B
Members	70,000
Date started	1981

Clay Pigeon Shooting Association (CPSA)

107 Epping New Road
Buckhurst Hill
Essex IG9 5TQ
Tel: (01) 505 6221

This is the governing body for the sport of clay pigeon shooting. The CPSA organises competitions, meetings, training and provides information for its members. Interested in knowing more? If so, write to the CPSA which will be pleased to help you.

Apply to	the address above
Age range	9–16
Joining fee	none
Annual fee	B
Members	10,578
Date started	1928

Muzzle Loaders' Association of Great Britain (MLAGB)

PO Box 217
Newport Pagnell
Buckinghamshire MK16 9YD

Shooting with muzzle loading pistols has become very popular since a large selection of reproduction weapons is now available. Flintlocks, percussion revolvers, duellers and target pistols, shot at twenty-five metres, and sometimes longer ranges, demand as much skill and practice to achieve success as the most modern handguns.

When you join the MLAGB you will be sent its annual magazine *Black Powder*, and regular newsletters, full of news, forthcoming events, and articles on topical and specialised subjects. It also holds four national clay competitions, together with local and regional clay shoots. Inter-branch matches are popular, and many members enjoy game, rough shooting and wildfowling with black powder guns. World Championships for muzzle loading weapons have been held since the early 1970s, and the MLAGB selects and sponsors the British team. There are also full pistol rifle and pistol competitions held each year.

There are over thirty branches of the Association throughout the United Kingdom each organising its own shooting events, social occasions and other activities. To find your nearest branch write to the MLAGB and ask for details.

Apply to	Mr W.S. Curtis, Honorary Treasurer, at the address above
Age range	15–16
Joining fee	A
Annual fee	B
Members	1,391
Date started	1952

National Small-Bore Rifle Association (NSRA)

Lord Robert's House
Bisley Camp
Brookwood
Woking
Surrey GU24 0NP
Tel: (04867) 6969

The NSRA promotes .22 target shooting and air weapon shooting. It organises exams and competitions, and provides its members with an information service. If you are thinking of joining a club, then the NSRA may well be able to put you in touch with one near to where you live.

Apply to	Mr John Pybus, at the address above
Age range	9–16
Joining fee	none
Annual fee	C
Members	41,000
Date started	1901

Scottish Clay Pigeon Association (SCPA)

2 Greengill
Gilcrux
Aspatria
Carlisle
Cumbria CA5 2RA
Tel: (0965) 21600

Living in Scotland and interested in clay pigeon shooting? The SCPA organises competitions, coachings, international matches, and provides members with an information service and a newsletter twice a year. It will be able to tell you where your nearest club meets.

Apply to	Mr Sandy Shiach, at the address above
Age range	further information on request
Joining fee	as above
Annual fee	as above
Members	782
Date started	1929

National Skating Association of Great Britain (NSA)

15–27 Gee Street
London EC1U 3RE
Tel: (01) 253 3824

Whether you are interested in roller speed or roller artistic skating, ice dancing, ice figure or ice speed skating the NSA has something to offer you. It organises training and competitions, and provides an information service for its members. If you want to know more write to the NSA, which will be pleased to help.

Apply to	the address above
Age range	9–16
Joining fee	C
Annual fee	none
Members	3,500
Date started	1879

Scottish Speed Skating Union (SSSU)

Hartley House
Racecourse View
Ayr KA7 2TX
Tel: (0292) 261081

If you want to take up amateur speed skating, and you live in Scotland write to the SSSU, which will be able to give you the address of your nearest club. You can then take part in competitions which the SSSU organises.

Apply to	the address above
Age range	9–16
Joining fee	none
Annual fee	B
Members	60
Date started	1949

Ski Club of Great Britain

118 Eaton Square
London SW1W 9AF
Tel: (01) 245 1033

Whether you can ski already, or want to learn, this Club has a great deal to offer. Advice is available on which equipment to buy, a wide range of which can be bought from the Club either by calling in or through mail order. Once you have your skis you can use the Club's equipment maintenance service.

Courses lasting one or two days on artificial dry slopes are run for members of intermediate or above standard. Skiing parties are organised for all ages and standards, with daily skiing to suit your ability. If you want to ski abroad you can book flights at very competitive prices.The Information Office holds full, up-to-date information on over 350 resorts, and there are Club representatives in over thirty major European resorts. If you want to check on the snow conditions before you leave for your holiday, the Club runs a 24-hour snow report service.

In addition over 350 discounts are available to members on goods and services, including holidays, throughout the UK and Europe. You can also choose from a wide range of books and information leaflets published by the Club, and five times a year you will receive the magazine *Ski Survey*.

Apply to	Miss Angela Bloomer, at the address above
Age range	9–16
Joining fee	D unless paying by direct debiting mandate
Annual fee	if living in London and 50 miles radius A, C if not
Members	18,500
Date started	1903

Scottish Ski Club (SSC)

Muircambus
Elie
Leven
Fife KY9 1HD
Tel: (033) 334200

You do not have to live in Scotland to join this Club, just interested in skiing. The SSC is at the front of junior racer training and it organises training schemes abroad and regular programmes in Scotland. Training grants and scholarships are also available to junior members.

During the summer, activities such as hill-walking, canoeing, golfing, windsurfing, gliding and hut work-party weekends are organised. Grass and artificial skiing and free-style events are organised by the SSC, together with a variety of races in which you can take part. A small selection of equipment, including normal skis for children, is available for hire.

Once a year you receive a magazine containing reports, photographs, and articles on all of the previous season's activities and races, and through the winter the newsletter *SSChuss* keeping you up-to-date with local activities and gossip.

Apply to	Jean Lindesay-Bethume, at the address above
Age range	9–16
Joining fee	none
Annual fee	C
Members	about 2,500
Date started	1907

Scottish Squash Rackets Association (SSRA)

18 Ainslie Place
Edinburgh EH3 6AU
Tel: (031) 225 2502

When you join this Association you receive a copy of the yearbook, newsletters and circulars on a wide variety of topics, and advance notice of all SSRA tournaments and courses. You can enter SSRA tournaments and other events and book seats at SSRA spectator events at special low prices before seats are put on sale to the general public. You also pay lower charges for SSRA Player Improvement Courses.

There is a range of books, posters and other goods free or for sale or hire available from the Association, as well as coaching services from SSRA trained and qualified coaches.

Apply to	the Secretary, at the address above
Age range	9–16
Joining fee	none
Annual fee	B
Members	about 500
Date started	1937

Squash Rackets Association (SRA)

Francis House
Francis Street
London SW1P 1DE
Tel: (01) 828 3064

According to the SRA, squash is the fastest growing sport in Britain, helping many to keep fit as well as to have fun. As a member of the SRA you can be a visiting member of more than three hundred squash clubs around Britain, have special priority booking rights for all the championships and tournaments, and receive automatic accident insurance when you are playing, training for matches or even watching squash. You will receive a free copy of the SRA *Annual* each October, giving all fixtures, facts, figures and results, and the magazine *Squash News*. There is a range of other publications, including a *Rules* poster for you to buy, together with a range of clothing all with the SRA logo.

Apply to	Mr Alan Chalmers, at the address above
Age range	9–16
Joining fee	none
Annual fee	B
Members	6,800
Date started	1928

Women's Squash Rackets Association (WSRA)

345 Upper Richmond Road West
London SW14 8QN
Tel: (01) 876 6219

If you are a girl and enjoy playing squash then you might like to find out more about this Association, which organises exams, competitions and provides its members with information.

Apply to	the address above
Age range	9–16
Joining fee	none
Annual fee	B
Members	2,040
Date started	1934

English Schools' Table Tennis Association (ESTTA)

'Engelberg'
Badger Lane
Woolley Moor
Derby DE5 6FG
Tel: (0246) 590164

Do you play table tennis at school? Is your school a member of a county association which is a member of ESTTA? If the answer to these two questions is 'yes', then you can take part in championships such as the Dunlop National School Team Championships, and the Dunlop Individual Championships, and receive training which this Association organises. There is also a Skills Award Scheme with five grades, 1, 2, 3, Matchplayer and Masters. Beginners start with Grade 1 and gradually work their way through each stage. Grades 1 and 2 emphasise tests which require a degree of touch, grade 3 introduces six more advanced tests, Matchplayer is designed for a good league player, and the Masters Award requires a high degree of skill as it includes control, spin and power. As you win an award you receive a woven badge and a certificate.

Apply to	Mr L.C. Henry, at the above address
Age range	9–16
Joining fee	none
Annual fee	paid by the schools
Members	50 county associations to which the schools belong
Date started	1968

English Table Tennis Association (ETTA)

21 Claremont
Hastings
East Sussex TN34 1HF
Tel: (0424) 433121

Wanting to know more about table tennis and clubs in England? Then write to this Association which will be pleased to help you.

Apply to	Mr A.W. Shipley, at the address above
Age range	9–16
Joining fee	none
Annual fee	A as a club member; D individual membership
Members	about 80,000
Date started	1927

Scottish Table Tennis Association (STTA)

18 Ainslie Place
Edinburgh EH3 6AU
Tel: (031) 225 3020

The STTA controls table tennis in Scotland. It organises competitions and training and provides its members with information. If you are thinking of taking up table tennis, and you live in Scotland, write and ask STTA for advice and information.

Apply to	the address above
Age range	further information on request
Joining fee	as above
Annual fee	as above
Members	2,500
Date started	1936

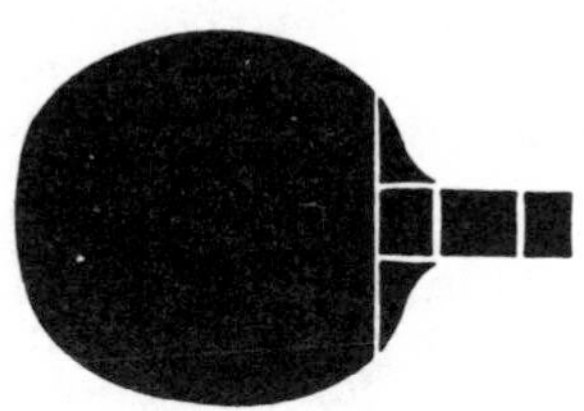

Table Tennis Association of Wales (TTAW)

198 Cyncoed Road
Cardiff CF2 6BQ
Tel: (0222) 757241

If you live in Wales and are interested in table tennis write to this Association for help, in finding a club to join, and for details of the competitions it organises.

Apply to	the address above
Age range	9–16
Joining fee	none
Annual fee	A and additional club membership
Members	3,000
Date started	1921

British Schools' Lawn Tennis Association

c/o The Lawn Tennis Foundation
Queen's Club
London W14 9EQ
Tel: (01) 385 4233

This Association aims to promote tennis in all schools. For a small annual subscription all schools can join, or if a school is already a member of a County Schools Tennis Association, it will automatically have membership of this national Association.

If your school is a member you will be able to take part in competitions, coaching courses, a badge award scheme for junior school children, and visits to Wimbledon. There are also regular information bulletins for you to read. National competitions include the Midland Bank/LTA Competition, which begins with local area leagues, the Nestlé Junior Tournament, which begins as a ladder tournament for individuals, the Midland Bank Glanvill (Boys) and Aberdare (Girls) Cups, which are team competitions for three doubles pairs, and the BSLTA Championships, played during a week in July.

Apply to	the address above
Age range	9–16
Joining fee	paid by the schools
Annual fee	paid by the schools
Members	about 1,500
Date started	1980

Lawn Tennis Association (LTA)

Barons Court
West Kensington
London W14 9EG
Tel: (01) 385 2366

Playing tennis can be good fun and the LTA will help you to get the most out of your game. It can tell you about the clubs in your area, and will advise on the equipment you need. Professional coaching is the best way to learn, and coaches can be found in clubs, parks, schools and sports centres. The LTA's handbook, *Tennis Great Britain*, lists their names and addresses, and the Association can advise you on the most suitable coaching for your needs.

If you cannot have professional coaching many local authorities run courses, including those for beginners, and some larger towns have a wider scope of tennis schemes. The Lawn Tennis Foundation, Queen's Club, London W14 9EQ can give you details. In addition there is an LTA/Prudential Junior Coaching Scheme for beginners aged eight to sixteen years, arranged each year in all counties. Most of the courses begin in April and May, and are held in parks or on school courts. Six hours of qualified instruction is offered at a modest fee. These courses are advertised at schools, libraries and sports centres, and further information is also available from the Lawn Tennis Foundation.

Apply to	Miss K.E. Tidmarsh, at the address above
Age range	9–16
Joining fee	none
Annual fee	B
Members	204,406
Date started	1888

Irish Lawn Tennis Association

22 Upper Fitzwilliam Street
Dublin 2

If you are interested in lawn tennis and living in Ireland write to this Association for information about clubs, coaching and competitions.

Apply to	the address above
Age range	further information on request
Joining fee	as above
Annual fee	as above
Members	as above

Scottish Lawn Tennis Association (SLTA)

12 Melville Crescent
Edinburgh EH3 7LV

If you live in Scotland and want to play lawn tennis the SLTA can help you find a club to join, and provide you with information about the game and the competitions and training it organises.

Apply to	the address above
Age range	9–16
Joining fee	paid by district associations
Annual fee	as above
Members	9 district associations
Date started	1895

Welsh Lawn Tennis Association (WLTA)

National Sports Centre for Wales
Sophia Gardens
Cardiff CF1 9SW
Tel: (0222) 371838

Living in Wales and wanting to join a tennis club? The WLTA can tell you which of its member clubs meets nearest to you. If you play tennis with your school club, this can also join the WLTA.

When a club belongs to this Association, its members can take part in tournaments and championships specially organised for juniors, such as the Nestlé Junior Tournament, the Prudential Welsh Junior Championships, the Colwyn Bay Open Junior Tournament, and the Mackintosh Open Junior Tournament. Some of these competitions take place on hard and covered courts. If you are a really good player you may be able to take part in international matches, too. The WLTA's handbook lists all of these competitions, together with a diary of events, and names and addresses of member clubs.

Apply to	the Honorary General Secretary, at the address above
Age range	9–16
Joining fee	paid by the clubs
Annual fee	paid by the clubs
Members	120 clubs, 3 associations

British Tenpin Bowling Association (BTBA)
19 Canterbury Avenue
Ilford
Essex IG1 3NA
Tel: (01) 554 9173

Do you go tenpin bowling? This Association has groups specially for younger members. It holds meetings, competitions and provides training advice and information. Write now and find out more.

Apply to	the address above
Age range	9–16
Joining fee	B
Annual fee	A
Members	40,000
Date started	1961

British Trampoline Federation Ltd (BTF)
152a College Road
Harrow HA1 1VH
Tel: (01) 863 7278

If you want to join a trampoline club write to the BTF for the address of your nearest one. You can also ask for information about the sport, training and competitions.

Apply to	the address above
Age range	further information on request
Joining fee	as above
Annual fee	as above
Members	as above
Date started	1965

Scottish Trampoline Association (STA)
18 Ainslie Place
Edinburgh EH3 6AU
Tel: (031) 226 4401

This is the national governing body for trampolining in Scotland. If this is your sport, then join the STA and take part in competitions. The Association can give you information, and will send you a newsletter six times a year.

Apply to	the address above
Age range	9–16
Joining fee	C
Annual fee	C
Members	about 300
Date started	1959

English Schools' Volleyball Association (ESVA)

4 High Trees House
Nightingale Lane
London SW12 8AQ
Tel: (01) 381 3606

If your school has a volleyball team it could be a member of this Association. Why not find out from your games teacher, because your team could be joining in competitions, training and other activities organised by ESVA?

Apply to	the address above
Age range	9–16
Joining fee	your school pays
Annual fee	your school pays
Members	about 250 schools
Date started	1968

English Volleyball Association (EVA)

13 Rectory Road
West Bridgford
Nottingham NG2 6BE
Tel: (0602) 816324

If you live in England and want to play volleyball this Association can provide information about local clubs, competitions and the game in general.

Apply to	the address above
Age range	further information on request
Joining fee	as above
Annual fee	as above
Members	6,048
Date started	1971

The Scottish Volleyball Association (SVA)

Castlecliff
25 Johnston Terrace
Edinburgh EH1 2NH
Tel: (031) 225 7311

Playing volleyball gives you fun, excitement, and the chance of skilful play as part of a team. With over a hundred million players worldwide and 150 national associations, volleyball can indeed be described as one of the most popular sports in the world today.

If you live in Scotland and your school or club joins the SVA, it will receive information about volleyball from rule books, teaching and coaching manuals, magazines, newsletters, books and charts all produced by the Association. Advice is available on which equipment to buy. As a player you will be able to take part in local competitions, and you may even play for the national squads and district representative teams taking part in national and international competitions.

Apply to	the address above
Age range	9–16
Joining fee	none
Annual fee	C
Members	2,147
Date started	1963

British Amateur Wrestling Association (BAWA)

16 Choir Street
Cambridge Industrial Estate
Salford M7 9ZD

If you want to take up wrestling, this Association, which is the governing body for amateur wrestling in England, Scotland, Wales and Northern Ireland, will be able to tell you where your nearest club meets and whom to contact. Once you are a member of a club you will be able to take part in tournaments, championships, such as the English Schoolboy Championships, and coaching schemes organised by the BAWA.

Apply to	Mr H.I. Jacob, OBE, at the address above
Age range	9–16
Joining fee	None
Annual fee	B
Members	6,000
Date started	1882

Scottish Amateur Wrestling Association (SAWA)

49 Brunstone Crescent
Joppa
Edinburgh
Tel: (031) 657 2383

If you live in Scotland and are interested in joining a wrestling club for coaching and taking part in competitions, then write to the SAWA which will be pleased to help you.

Apply to	the address above
Age range	further information on request
Joining fee	as above
Annual fee	as above
Members	320
Date started	1930

12

Water Sports

CANOEING

British Canoe Union
45–47 High Street
Addlestone
Weybridge
Surrey KT15 1JV
Tel: (0932) 41341/2

The canoe was the first true boat (excepting rafts and floats) to be built by primitive man. It has been used in every part of the world and some canoes have been found dating back to the Stone Age. Native canoes are still used for transport and hunting, but now canoeing is a popular sport, which was introduced to the world by the Scottish sportsman and traveller John MacGregor in the 1860s.

The British Canoe Union is the national body governing canoeing with specialist groups for sprint racing, marathon, slalom, canoe sailing, wild water racing, surf, canoe polo, sea canoeing, coaching and the Corps of Canoe Lifeguard.

The Union organises exhibitions, conferences, visits and excursions. Members receive a magazine *Canoe Focus* six times a year, and are able to buy other helpful publications such as the *Canoeing Directory.* As a member you also receive an automatic licence to use the British Waterways Board's waters and third party insurance. There is also low-cost canoe insurance.

Apply to	the address above
Age range	9–16
Joining fee	none
Annual fee	B (first year only); then C
Members	13,150
Date started	1936

Scottish Canoe Association (SCA)

18 Ainslie Place
Edinburgh EH3 6AU
Tel: (031) 226 4401

The SCA is the governing body for canoeing in Scotland. As a member you can take part in events including slalom, touring, long-distance racing, surfing, canoe surfing, white water racing, sprint, marathon racing and bat polo. The Association also organises meeting and administers tests for proficiency certificates. A quarterly newsletter will keep you up-to-date with news and forthcoming events. You can buy a number of very helpful books and guides published by the SCA and members may borrow videos on various aspects of canoeing.

Apply to the Administrator, at the address above
Age range 9–16
Joining fee none
Annual fee C
Members 1,490
Date started 1939

The Surf Life-Saving Association of Great Britian (SLSA of GB)

4 Cathedral Yard
Exeter EX1 1HJ
Tel: (0392) 54364

Life-saving is a recreational activity, a competitive sport and a community service. There are 52 clubs in this Association, grouped into 4 regions. Members of the SLSA of GB patrol Britain's beaches in their own time at their own expense. Activities vary from beach patrolling to rescuing people in danger of drowning, from basic first aid to advanced resuscitation, from training for general fitness to qualify for proficiency awards, from beach sprints to long distance surf ski races, and from paddling surf craft to power boating. Taking part helps you to keep fit, and to develop your swimming and life-saving skills.

You do not have to be able to swim to join this Association as there is always help required in 'back room' jobs, including fund raising.

Apply to Mr R.G. Ferguson, National Secretary, at the address above
Age range older readers
Joining fee none
Annual fee as a member of a Surf Life-Saving Club you are also a member of SLSA of GB
Members 3,500
Date started 1955

Amateur Rowing Association Limited (ARA)

6 Lower Mall
London W6 9DJ
Tel: (01) 748 3632

If you are interested in rowing the ARA will be able to tell you where your nearest club meets and whom to contact. Once a member of a club you will be able to take part in ARA organised competitions.

Apply to	the address above
Age range	older readers
Annual fee	paid by your club
Members	1,650
Date started	1882

Scottish Amateur Rowing Association Limited (SARA)

10 Kip Avenue
Inverkip by Greenock
Renfrewshire PA16 0DX
Tel: (0475) 520117

Rowing is an excellent sport if you want to develop strength, stamina, speed and mental determination, as well as have a good deal of fun.

In Scotland many people enjoy this sport in the main rowing areas of Aberdeen, Edinburgh, Stirling, Loch Lomond, Glasgow, Dumfries, Greenock and Lochwinnoch. Write for the name and address of the organiser of your local club.

Apply to	Mr Stewart Bates, at the address above
Age range	9–16
Joining fee	none
Annual fee	paid by clubs
Members	130 clubs
Date started	1881

Association of Sea Training Organisations

c/o RYA
Victoria Way
Woking
Surrey GU21 1EQ
Tel: (048 62) 5022

This Association brings together the many independent organisations which offer young people sail training and adventure at sea. Members include: the Ocean Youth Club offering weekend, one week and longer courses in eight 72ft ketches, one 50ft gaff yawl, one 55ft yawl, one 76ft gaff ketch, and one 70ft replica pilot schooner, for boys and girls aged twelve to twenty-four; the Island Cruising Club with one week or longer cruises on various yachts 26ft to 72ft, dinghies and keel boats for boys and girls from ten years of age; the London Sailing Project offering three-day weekend and six-day cruises for boys from fifteen years of age, living in London, on three ketches; the East Coast Sail Trust offering five-day cruises on a 91ft seagoing spritsail barge for girls and boys from eleven years of age. If you would like to take part in these and other exciting experiences, then write to the Association for further information.

Apply to	the address above
Age range	10–16
Date started	1971

National School Sailing Association (NSSA)

Erw-Fair
Marton Cum Grafton
York YO5 9QY
Tel: (09012) 2818

The NSSA advises schools and youth clubs on how to set up and organise sailing training schemes. Once your club or school is a member, you can take part in a national proficiency scheme, and eventually even compete in a team championship. By the time you have reached a good level of competence you can attend special advanced level courses for young people, also organised by the NSSA.

The NSSA keeps you informed through sending its members a handbook, newsletter, and a list of pamphlets which you can obtain on such things as safety and insurance.

Apply to	Mr D.G. Sykes, at the address above
Age range	9–16
Joining fee	none
Annual fee	the school or club pays
Members	1,000
Date started	1958

Royal Yachting Association (RYA)

RYA House
Romsey Road
Eastleigh
Hampshire SO5 4YA
Tel: (0703) 629962

When you join the Royal Yachting Association you can choose, for free, books from the Association worth over half your subscription fee. A list of titles, which includes books not published by the RYA, is sent to you, and extra titles will be offered in the free annual catalogue and the quarterly magazine *The RYA News.* You are given a personal sail number, and have the pleasure and convenience of using your own special lounge and restaurant at the London Boat Show. You can use the free enquiry service which replies to you by return of post, and further information can be found in the hundreds of factual sheets which the RYA produces for its members.

The RYA has more than 1,000 recognised and regularly inspected teaching establishments in the United Kingdom, which offer courses such as the Basic Sailing Award, the National Dinghy Certificate, and a special certificate which can lead to Olympic selection for juniors. If you enjoy racing, the RYA organises youth championships in which you can compete.

Apply to	Membership Manager, at the address above
Age range	9–16
Joining fee	none
Annual fee	B
Members	53,815
Date started	1875

British Surfing Association (BSA)

G5 Burrows Chambers
East Burrows Road
Swansea
West Glamorgan SA1 1RF
Tel: (0792) 461476

Surfing began in the Polynesian Islands of the Pacific Ocean and is enjoyed by millions of young people worldwide. It has grown in popularity in Britain over recent years. When you join the BSA you receive a membership card, newsletters on surfing developments and activities at home and abroad, including entry forms for major contests such as the English National and Great Britain Championships held each year. Third party insurance cover, which is required at many British beaches, is offered at a specially low price. You can also obtain free leaflets on many aspects of surfing, a list of surf shops, a list of surfing beaches in Britain, a booklist, and a list of surf clubs which are members of the BSA.

Apply to	Mr Mike Cunningham, at the address above
Age range	9–16
Joining fee	none
Annual fee	B
Members	526
Date started	1968

Amateur Swimming Association (ASA)

Harold Fern House
Derby Square
Loughborough
Leicestershire LE11 0AL
Tel: (0509) 230431

If you are interested in swimming, diving, water polo or synchronised swimming the ASA, which is the Association which governs these, can give you the address of your nearest club. There are 1,760 swimming clubs which are members of the ASA. Once you have joined a club you can start to enjoy the benefits of the ASA — the awards scheme, a magazine called *The Swimming Times*, and the 'Learn to Swim' schemes.

Apply to	Mr D. A. Reeves, the Secretary, at the address above
Age range	9–16
Annual fee	paid by the clubs
Members	1,760
Date started	1869

Channel Swimming Association (CSA)

Sunnybank
Alkham Valley Road
Folkestone
Kent CT18 7EH
Tel: (0303) 892229

Planning to swim the English Channel? If so you must be registered with this Association. Not only will you receive advice and useful information, but it is the

CSA which authenticates your claim to have succeeded in your swim. You can obtain information on weather conditions, tides, hazards in the Channel, and Channel swimming rules. This and a good deal more is available in an information pack which can be bought from the CSA. It is also possible to buy a handbook, and you will receive a newsletter once a year.

Apply to	Mrs Audrey Scott, Honorary Secretary at the address above
Age range	older readers
Joining fee	none
Annual fee	B
Members	200
Date started	1927

English Schools' Swimming Association (ESSA)

3 Maybank Grove
Liverpool L17 6DW
Tel: (051) 427 3707

The ESSA promotes swimming, diving, water polo, synchronised swimming and life-saving for school children to learn and enjoy. Your swimming club or school can join this Association if it is in England and then you will be able to take part in competitions. If you want to join a club, ESSA can tell you where your nearest club meets and who to contact.

Apply to	the address above
Age range	9–16
Joining fee	paid by your club or school
Date started	1949

National Association of Swimming Clubs for the Handicapped (NASCH)

219 Preston Drive
Brighton BN1 6FL
Tel: (0273) 559470

If you are handicapped and would like to join a club which specially meets your swimming needs then write to this Association, which will be pleased to let you know where your nearest club meets. NASCH also organises competitions in which you can take part.

Apply to	the address above
Age range	9–16
Annual fee	paid by the club
Members	100 clubs
Date started	1965

Scottish Amateur Swimming Association (SASA)

Pathfoot Building
University of Stirling
Stirling FK9 4LA

Living in Scotland and wanting to join a swimming club? Then write to SASA which will tell you where your local club meets.

Apply to	the address above
Age range	9–16
Joining fee	none
Annual fee	B for 11–16 year olds
Members	17,500
Date started	1888

Scottish Schools' Swimming Association (SSSA)

7 Ardross Court
Glenrothes
Fife

If your school is in Scotland it can join the SSSA, and you can then take part in competitions which the Association organises. Want to know more? If so, see if your school is a member, and if not ask your swimming teacher to write to SSSA for more information.

Apply to	the address above
Age range	9–16
Annual fee	your school pays
Members	12 regions
Date started	1950

Welsh Amateur Swimming Association (WASA)

National Sports Centre for Wales
Sophia Gardens
Cardiff CF1 9SW
Tel: (0222) 397571

WASA is the Association to contact if you live in Wales and are interested in joining a swimming, diving or water polo club. It will be able to tell you where your nearest club meets so that you can enjoy your sport, and even take part in championships organised by the WASA.

Apply to	Miss O. Jones, 18 Station Road, Mochdre, Colwyn Bay, Clwyd
Age range	9–16
Annual fee	paid by the clubs
Members	9,000
Date started	1897

British Water-Ski Federation (BWSF)

390 City Road
London EC1V 2QA
Tel: (01) 833 2855

This is the governing body for water-skiing in the United Kingdom, organising coaching, exhibitions, meetings and competitions. The BWSF will be able to tell you, amongst other things, where your nearest club meets and whom to contact if you want to join.

Apply to	the Secretary at the address above
Age range	9–16
Joining fee	further information on request
Annual fee	C individual membership; D family membership
Members	about 11,000
Date started	1949

NOTES

13

Technical

ASTRONOMY

The British Astronomical Association (BAA)

Burlington House
Piccadilly
London W1V 0NL
Tel: (01) 734 4145

Do you enjoy observing the sky at night, and would you like to contribute to the scientific study of stars and planets? If so, the BAA is keen to encourage all aspects of observational astronomy, and to bring together those involved in the observation of the sky. It does not matter if you are a beginner, you will be welcome as a member, and given the opportunity to join one or more of the following sections: Sun, Moon, Terrestrial Planets (Mercury, Venus, Mars, and minor planets), Jupiter, Saturn, Comets, Meteors, Variable Stars, Deep Sky (double stars, galactic, and extra galactic objects), Aurora, Artificial Satellites, Historical, Computing and Observing Techniques (including radio and electronics). Each section is supervised by an experience director, who gives members advice and suggests programmes of work for them to undertake. Other interests are covered by less formal groups, including a micro-computer users' group.

As a member of BAA you will receive, six times a year, a magazine with articles and reports of members' observations, together with reviews of new books. An annual handbook including day-to-day information to help with observational work, will be sent to you. If you pay a small additional subscription you receive circulars giving immediate notification of special events, such as the discovery of a comet or nova. Other publications are available for you to buy, such as star charts, posters and other special booklets. Most sections issue newsletters, and many provide information sheets on specific topics. You will receive invitations to meetings, and a number of residential weekend courses are organised each year. There are over three hundred instruments for loan to members, and a specialist library from which you can borrow.

Apply to	the Assistant Secretary, at the address above
Age range	older readers
Joining fee	A
Annual fee	D
Members	3,330
Date started	1890

Junior Astronomical Society (JAS)

10 Swanwick Walk
Tadley
Basingstoke
Hampshire RG26 6JZ

When setting out to explore a new interest it is always useful to join a club or society which aims to help beginners. Such is the Junior Astronomical Society. Anyone can take up astronomy; all you need is a pair of binoculars and a star map, and by joining this Society you can learn what to look for, and be kept up-to-date with developments in the sky and space. You will receive *Popular Astronomy* which is full of articles, information on developments in space research, a computer column, reviews of new books and telescopes, and a Sky Diary telling you what you can look out for.

Regular meetings are held, though mainly in London, where you can hear talks by the country's top astronomers, and meet fellow enthusiasts. There is a popular weekend course normally held each year, providing the opportunity to compare different telescopes, observe faint objects which you may not be able to see at home, hear interesting talks and take part in a range of activities. Visits are also made to research centres such as Jodrell Bank and the Mullard Observatory at Cambridge.

Like the British Astronomical Association, the JAS has observing sections — Aurora, Comets, Deep Sky, Lunar, Meteor, Occultations, Photography, Planetary, Satellite, Solar and Variable Stars. These are run by experienced observers who are happy to provide interesting projects and give advice.

Apply to	the Secretary at the address above
Age range	9–16
Joining fee	none
Annual fee	C
Members	1,672
Date started	1953

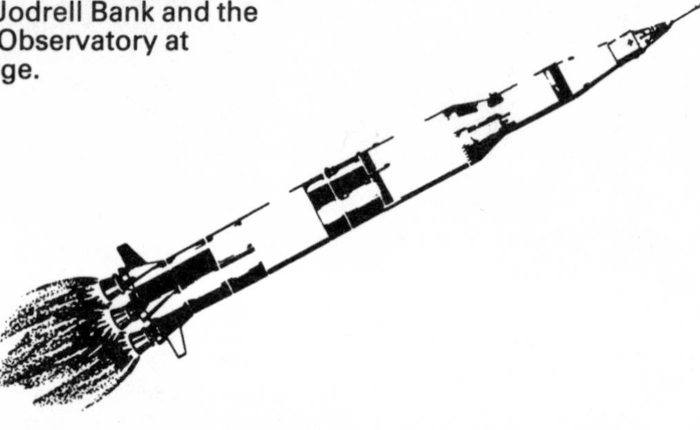

The Association of 16mm Narrow Gauge Modellers

'Pipers'
Fields Road
Chedworth
Cheltenham
Gloucestershire GL54 4NQ
Tel: (028 572) 677

Are you interested in modelling on a large scale? Operating live steam locomotives? A model railway in your own garden? Have you considered narrow gauge model railways in the scale 16mm : 1ft on 0 gauge (32mm) track giving a prototype 2ft narrow gauge system? Modelling on this large scale need be no more expensive than working 'OO' or 'N' gauges. As little as £10 could get you started.

This Association has many members with their own outdoor narrow gauge railway and a few even have room for an indoor layout as well! Membership is open to all, even those who are unable to have a layout of their own. When you join this Association you will receive a quarterly magazine and will be invited to garden meetings throughout the summer, indoor winter meetings, and specialist sales including precision components, kits, O gauge items for conversion, materials, books and even members' unwanted models.

Apply to	Mr Edward Hodson, 25 Norman Road, Tall Trees, Penkridge, Staffordshire ST19 5EX
Age range	9–16
Joining fee	none
Annual fee	C
Date started	1977

British Slot Car Racing Association (BSCRA)

6 Cedar Road
Balby
Doncaster DN4 9JT
Tel: (0302) 851178

Slot car racing is here with a vengeance. Since its humble beginnings with Scalextrix cars, the serious side of the sport has developed to the stage where cars can reach 50 mph, and can out-accelerate a real Formula One car. The cars are built to 1/32 scale, the average being 5 inches long and 2½ inches wide. All models look like full-size racing cars, and racing is divided into three main classes — Grand Prix, Sports and GT cars, and Saloon cars.

The BSCRA controls slot car racing in Britain, promotes the sport, organises area and national championship racing, and administers car regulations. It publishes a handbook and a magazine, *Slot Car Racing*, which members receive every two months.

If you want to take part in this exciting hobby, then write to BSCRA's secretary at the address above and ask for details of your nearest club.

Apply to	Mr M. Roberts, Membership Secretary, at the above address
Age range	9–16
Joining fee	none
Annual fee	B; club members 9–15; club members 16, B
Members	331
Date started	1964

The Miniature Armoured Fighting Vehicles (AFV) Association (MAFVA)

15 Berwick Avenue
Heaton Mersey
Stockport
Cheshire SK4 3AA
Tel: (061) 432 7574

This Association encourages interest in armoured fighting vehicles (AFV) and their equipment. It also collects and provides information, trying to answer questions and looking for sources of information for its fast-growing membership. Members' interests range from the First World War to the present day, although the greatest emphasis is centred around the Second World War. Most members make and/or collect models, though there are many who collect information only.

If you join the MAFVA you will receive, every two months, the magazine, *Tankette,* containing articles, with drawings and photographs, about tanks, self-propelled guns, ½-tracks, armoured cars, trucks, artillary, uniforms, unit organisation, vehicle colour schemes and marking, kit conversions, histories, scratch building projects, and tips and kit and book reviews. Each issue also contains several multi-view original scale plans. There are meetings, displays and competitions, and a unique range of 1/76th kits for you to collect.

Apply to	Mr A. Leese, Membership Secretary, at the above address
Age range	9–16
Joining fee	none
Annual fee	B; club members 9–15; club members 16, B
Members	331
Date started	1964

The Model Railway Club (MRC)

Keen House
4-8 Calshot Street
London N1 9DA
Tel: (01) 833 1840

Whilst anyone with an interest in model railways can join this Club, if you live in London you have additional benefits. All members can enjoy the annual International Model Railway Exhibition which is the largest and oldest model railway show in the United Kingdom. There is also a regular Club bulletin, full of articles and reports, together with letters, notices and reviews. At the MRC headquarters, in London, meetings are held every Thursday evening. During the winter, the third meeting in the

month generally includes a lecture or presentation connected with prototype or model railways. The other Thursdays are 'track nights' when members come in to run models on the test tracks, browse in the library, work on modelling projects, or just to gossip about their hobby. There are also occasional Saturday open days.

Everyone is welcome to join this Club, even those who are just starting out in this interesting hobby. If you are interested and live in London pop into Keen House one Thursday evening — visitors are warmly welcomed. Otherwise, write to the Club and ask for more information.

Apply to	Mr J.E. Geach, at the address above
Age range	9–16
Joining fee	none
Annual fee	C (B if 35 miles from Charing Cross)
Members	350
Date started	1910

Scottish Aeromodellers' Association (SAA)

6 Crookston Path
Glasgow G52 3LN
Tel: (041) 883 2655

Aeromodelling is one of the most creative and interesting sports, in which you will be able to learn a variety of skills in constructing and operating models. Whether you are interested in control-line models, free-flight models or radio-controlled models including soarers, the SAA can help you.

Throughout Scotland there are around forty clubs which are members of the SAA. By joining one of these clubs you will receive expert help and advice. The SAA can tell you where your nearest club meets.

Apply to	Mr T. Gray, at the address above
Age range	9–16
Joining fee	none
Annual fee	A
Members	1,050
Date started	1944

Society of Model Aeronautical Engineers (SMAE)

3rd Floor
Kimberley House
47 Vaughan Way
Leicester
Tel: (0533) 58500

Interested in model aircraft flying? If so, this Society is working hard for you — preserving and buying flying fields, obtaining radio-control frequencies, providing a code of practice of model aircraft noise, and taking an interest in safety and heavy models, such as quarter scale.

Most members are not contest-minded; others take a more active part in the wide range of activities the Society offers. These members enjoy taking part in local, national, and international competitions. Some members even represent Britain at world championships.

Membership includes free third party insurance as well as special cover for flying on Ministry of Defence airfields. When you join SMAE you receive a handbook, which includes information on safety, noise, insurance, byelaws and the popular R/C Achievement Scheme. This Scheme is a simple two-stage pilot's aptitude test for glider or power flyers, for which SMAE awards silver or gold wings, proudly worn by almost 2,000 R/C flyers.

Control-line radio-controlled flying, radio-controlled soaring, free-flight and scale flying rule books may be purchased by members at reduced prices — just one more service offered by this Society. There are about 350 clubs in Britain with members in SMAE, so write today and find out where your nearest club meets.

Apply to	Mrs Margaret Orton, at the address above
Age range	9–16
Joining fee	none
Annual fee	B
Members	13,300
Date started	1922

Radio Society of Great Britain (RSGB)

Lambda House
Cranborne Road
Potters Bar
Hertfordshire EN6 3JE
Tel: (0707) 59015

Amateur radio is a unique hobby which puts hundreds of thousands of people all over the world into direct contact with each other every day. There are over one and a half million licensed amateur radio enthusiasts in the world in just about every country, all operating their stations from home.

When you join the RSGB you can ask for information and advice, and use the special library. There are competitions for you to enter and exams you can take to learn more about your hobby. Once a month you will receive *Radio Communication*, a magazine, and once a year the *Amateur Radio Call Book*. The Society also publishes other useful books and guides for you to buy.

Apply to	the New Member Dept, at the address above
Age range	9–16
Joining fee	none
Annual fee	C
Members	34,000
Date started	1913

Irish Radio Transmitters' Society (IRTS)

PO Box 462
Dublin 9

Radio amateurs fall into two broad types — those who are involved through their jobs in the radio and electronics industries, and those who are not. The IRTS is the national society in Ireland which represents these radio amateurs. As a member you will receive a monthly newsletter, a 'QSL' or radio contact confirmation card exchange service, weekly transmitted news bulletins, access to technical journals and the opportunity to take part in various activities such as lectures, field days, expeditions to offshore islands, and social events. Each year awards are made to members who have, for example, displayed operating proficiency under contest conditions. The Society also holds classes in radio theory and morse code at centres in Dublin, and in some country areas local radio clubs hold similar courses for beginners.

Apply to	the address above
Age range	9–16
Joining fee	none
Annual fee	C
Members	600
Date started	1932

Use this letter as a guide if you want to write to a national organisation to find out if there is a branch or affiliated club near you. Address your letter to The Secretary, and don't forget to include your own name and address.

Dear Sir (or Madam)

My hobby is   and I would like to find a local club that I can join. Could you please send me details of any that are near where I live? I enclose a stamped addressed envelope for your reply. Thank you.

I found your address in *Where to Join.*

Yours faithfully

14

Transport

AIRSHIPS

Airship Association

3 Chestnut Avenue
East Sheen
London SW14 8NT
Tel: (01) 876 7046

The first successful airship took to the skies in 1852, and since then airships have been used to explore the North Pole, provide a trans-atlantic passenger service, carry bombs (the infamous Zeppelins), and provide anti-submarine patrols in wartime. However, as these airships were filled with hydrogen, there were many accidents. This Association believes that today's safer designs, using non-inflammable helium, means that airships can provide a useful service carrying freight, undertaking coastal patrols and survey work, and acting as ferries. The Airship Association has a worldwide membership interested in the future of airships, and is in close contact with all who are studying, building and promoting airships.

If you have an interest in airships, and would like to see them used more, then join this Association. You will receive a quarterly magazine *Airship*, which includes news, comments, book reviews and articles on airships. You will be invited to meetings and lectures all concerned with the future of the modern airship.

Apply to	the address above
Age range	older readers
Joining fee	none
Annual fee	B
Members	245
Date started	1971

The Omnibus Society (OS)

15 Sutton Court
Little Sutton Lane
Sutton Coldfield
West Midlands B75 6SE
Tel: (021) 355 1132

Whilst some people see buses on our roads solely as a means of getting from one place to another, the OS sees them as a hobby, together with coaches, trolley buses and tramcars.

If you join OS you will receive *The Omnibus Magazine*, four times a year, which includes feature articles, operational and general news, and details of meetings and visits. There is a well-established network of branches throughout the United Kindom, each with a full programme of activities. In the winter, indoor informal meetings are held, including film and slide shows, discussions and talks. In the summer, visits and tours are arranged to bus operators and manufacturers.

The Society has lending and reference libraries for the use of members, together with a Ticket Collection and a Timetable Collection. Further information is available from the Society's special publications, dealing with particular aspects of the history or development of the bus industry.

Apply to	the Membership Registrar, at the address above
Age range	13–16
Joining fee	A
Annual fee	D (B without magazine)
Members	1,030
Date started	1929

Hoverclub of Great Britain Limited (HCGB)

10 Long Acre
Bingham
Nottingham NG13 8BG
Tel: (0949) 37294

Through this Club people of all ages who are interested in building and operating light hovercraft are brought together. If you or your school is thinking about building a hovercraft, then by joining this Club you will be able to save time and money through sharing information which the other members have collected over the years.

The HCGB organises pleasure cruising, hover holidays, and the very competitive national racing series held each year. Local branches of the HCGB hold monthly meetings to discuss the building and use of hovercraft, and as a member you will be able to go along to these. You will also be able to buy publications about building light hovercraft, and get information on regulations. All members receive a monthly magazine, *Light Hovercraft*, which contains useful constructional advice, news, and dates and places of local meetings.

With ever-increasing costs of materials and engines it is wise to seek advice on what to use and where to obtain materials. This Club can provide you proven plans, as well as completed new craft, advice and information.

Apply to	Mrs D. Naylor, 12 Mount Pleasant, Bishops Itchington, Leamington Spa, Warwickshire, CU33 0BE Tel: (0926) 613180
Age range	older readers
Joining fee	none
Annual fee	C
Members	480
Date started	1967

Inland Waterways' Association (IWA)

114 Regent's Park Road
London NW1 8UQ
Tel: (01) 586 2510/2556

Did you know that there are 3,000 miles of navigable waterways in Britain? That 990 miles are in commercial use? That there are 1,400 locks in use in Britain? That the longest canal tunnel, Standedge on the Huddersfield Narrow Canal, is 3¼ miles long? That the longest aqueduct is Pontycysyllte, 303.3m long, carrying the Llangollen Canal 36.7m above the River Dee? Are you interested in boating, angling, rambling, watching wildlife, conservation, transport by water or the restoration of derelict waterways? If you answer 'yes' to one or more of these questions, then this Association may well be what you are looking for.

When you join the IWA you receive the magazine *Waterways*, which includes news and information on local events for your area. You can go to meetings, talks, and film shows organised by your local branch. Waterway rallies are held throughout Britain, and you can spend your weekends in 'digs' restoring canals.

Apply to	the address above
Age range	9–16
Joining fee	none
Annual fee	B
Members	20,150
Date started	1946

Great Western Society (GWS)

Didcot Railway Centre
Didcot
Oxfordshire OX11 7NJ
Tel: (0235) 817200

The Great Western Railway was created by an Act of Parliament over 150 years ago, and thanks to this Society there is still some of it to see operating today.

The GWS has taken over the locomotive depot and surrounding area at Didcot in Oxfordshire and transformed it into the Didcot Railway Centre. Restored Great Western trains are operated on two demonstration lines, and a typical station with a working signalbox and signalling has been created. A carriage shed has been erected, the turntable replaced, as Brunel's broad gauge railway has been revived. All of this is the result of hardwork from member volunteers. As a member living near Didcot you too can take an active part in locomotive or carriage restoration, track laying, or other engineering activities. It does not matter if you are unskilled. If you do not live near the Centre, you can still become a member of the GWS, able to attend branch meetings in various parts of the country, and support the work at Didcot through your membership.

When you join the GWS you receive eight newsletters a year and the illustrated magazine *Great Western Echo*, published quarterly, provides features on the GWR. You also get priority booking and fare reduction on the Society's steam railtours on the main line.

Apply to	Mr Brian Philips, at the address above
Age range	9–16
Joining fee	A
Annual fee	B
Members	4,350
Date started	1961

Railway Correspondence and Travel Society (RCTS)

Dept 0
160 Hillend Crescent
Clarkston
Renfrewshire G76 7XY
Tel: (021) 565 3333

The aims of this Society are to increase interest in railways, and to provide opportunities for members to study various aspects of railway history, operation and development. There are nineteen branches throughout Britain, each of which holds regular meetings, to which guest speakers are invited. Slide shows and other activities are also organised. Branches arrange visits to works, depots, and other places of railway interest. When you join the RCTS you receive an illustrated monthly magazine, *The Railway Observer*, which provides details of these meetings and visits together with sections on locomotive allocations, stock alterations, current news, coaching, freight and departmental stock, overseas railways, preservation notes, works news, historical and technical articles and reviews.

The Society arranges rail tours, and usually you can pay lower fares for these. Visits to the railways of Europe and elsewhere are also a regular feature of each year's activities.

If you wish to read about your hobby, the Society produces a series of publications which you can buy at special low prices, and operates a large library from which you can borrow.

Apply to	the address above
Age range	14–16 but you must be supported by an existing member
Joining fee	none
Annual fee	C
Members	about 6,000
Date started	1928

World Ship Society (WSS)

35 Wickham Way
Haywards Heath
West Sussex RH16 1UJ
Tel: (0444) 413066

If you are interested in ships and shipping the WSS has a good deal to offer you. It is the leading organisation catering for the needs of ship enthusiasts everywhere, with members in more than fifty countries.

When you join the WSS you receive the monthly magazine *Marine News*, which provides full news of naval and merchant ships throughout the world, as well as interesting articles and information about branch activities. The Society has made a large collection of reference books, and it also possesses one of the world's major collections of ship photographs from which you can buy prints.

Throughout Britain there are branches which usually have meetings once a month, at which you will be able to hear talks, see films and slide shows, take part in occasional competitions and quizzes, or just talk about ships. In addition, visits are arranged to ships and dock installations, and there are occasional cruises and short sea trips. Some branches publish their own magazine and newsletters.

Anyone interested in ships can join the WSS. Some of its members are still at school like you.

Apply to	WSS, 58 Bicton Street, Exmouth, Devon, EX8 2RU
Age range	9–16
Joining fee	none
Annual fee	D
Members	3,852
Date started	1946

Road Roller Society (RRA)

32 Grampian Road
Little Sandhurst
Camberley
Surrey

The earliest known steam rollers were made in France in 1860. The first to be made in England was built in 1863 for use in India, and Thomas Aveling produced his first rollers in 1865. Developments continued in England, France and the USA, and by 1880 the familiar three-wheel form of steam roller existed.

The RRA encourages the preservation of road rollers, living vans, water carts, tar boilers, and other equipment used for road construction. When you join this Association you receive the quarterly magazine *Rolling*, which includes news, articles, and a small ads section. Social activities and roller workings are held in various parts of Britain from time to time. The Association also has a reference library, and various books and other publications are available for you to buy. A useful booklet for enthusiasts is one which lists known rollers 'parked up' in parks, playgrounds and museums, published by the RRA. Registers of motor rollers and roller living vans are being compiled now.

Apply to	Mr P. Knight 22 Rowditch Avenue, Derby
Age range	9–16
Joining fee	none
Annual fee	B
Members	269
Date started	1974

Tramway and Light Railway Society (TLRS)

6 The Woodlands
Brightlingsea
Colchester
Essex CO7 0RY

This is the Society to join if you are interested in any aspect of tramways and light railways — even modelling them. As a member you will be able to go to meetings and exhibitions, and to get information about your hobby. Four times a year you will receive the *Tramfare,* an illustrated bi-monthly magazine giving you plenty to read and up-to-date information.

Apply to	the address above
Age range	9–16
Joining fee	none
Annual fee	B
Members	520
Date started	1938

British Trolleybus Society (BTS)

8 Reeds Avenue
Earley
Reading RG6 2SR

The BTS not only studies the history and development of the trolleybus as a form of transport, but also supports its being brought back into service. So if you are a trolleybus admirer join this Society so that you can support its work, attend meetings, and use its library and information service. As a member you will receive the monthly magazines *Trolleybus* and *Busfare*.

Apply to	the address above
Age range	further information on request
Joining fee	as above
Annual fee	as above
Members	377
Date started	1961

Trolleybus Museum Company (TMC)

29A Hillfield Park
London N10 3QT
Tel: (01) 883 3202

The TMC studies and writes about trolleybus operation and is interested in preserving old trolleybuses. If you join, there are meetings and exhibitions to attend, visits and excursions to take part in, and an information service for you to call upon. Six times a year the TMC publishes the *Trolleybus Magazine* which you can buy for a small subscription.

Apply to	the address above
Age range	9–16
Joining fee	none
Annual fee	C
Members	453
Date started	1963

15

Miscellaneous

BATON-TWIRLING

National Baton Twirling Association (NBTA)

PO Box 21
Newton Abbot
Devon
Tel: (06267) 3741

Have you ever been to a summer fête and seen a smart troupe of girls and boys marching or dancing to music skilfully twirling batons up into the air and catching them again? Well such a troupe is likely to belong to the NBTA, which promotes competitions in baton twirling. Members include young people in majorette corps, whether these are marching bands, pom pom groups, military marching groups or parade formation corps.

The NBTA organises meetings, training, regional and national competitions, and also is involved in world championships. Four times a year members receive *Twirling UK*, an attractive magazine full of news, photographs, articles, letters and information on competitions and special events.

Apply to	Mr K.W. Gill, Secretary, Comilla, Higher Buckeridge, Teignmouth, Devon
Age range	9–16
Joining fee	B
Annual fee	C
Members	4,500
Date started	1973

BOARD GAMES

British Go Association (BGA)

The Hollies
Wollerton
Market Drayton
Shropshire TF9 3LY
Tel: (0630) 84292

Go is a game of territory. The Go board is marked with a grid of nineteen lines by nineteen lines, and can be thought of as a piece of land to be shared between two players. One player has a large number of black discs, known as stones, and the other a large supply of white stones. Starting with an empty board, the players take turns to move by placing their stones on the crossing points of the lines on the board. The players usually start by staking out their claims to different areas of the board which they eventually intend to surround and control. Enemy stones can be surrounded and captured, but each player's main aim is to be the one with the greater total area under his or her command at the end of the game.

Go probably began in central Asia and then spread eastwards. There are ancient records of Go in both Nepal and Tibet, and from there the game reached China. Evidence of Go, or Wei-chii as the Chinese called it, has been traced as early as 2356 BC. Finally the game reached Japan around 500 AD, and grew to become Japan's most popular board game. It was not until 1880 that Go was played in Europe, and finally reached Britain about 1930.

The BGA promotes the game of Go within the British Isles, and anyone can join. As a member you receive a newsletter six times a year and the *British Go Journal* four times a year. There are also meetings and competitions in which you can take part. The setting up of Go clubs, including those based in schools, is encouraged and special starter packages are sent to these new clubs, along with equipment on loan. There is a very large programme of Go tournaments, and two trust funds, the Castledine Trust and the Susan Barnes' Trust, exist to promote the playing of Go by young people.

Go demands great skill, strategy and patience, yet the rules and pieces are so simple that young children can play. Special handicap rules exist so that players of unequal skill can play together, and even if you are a beginner you can still join in.

Apply to	Mr B.C. Timmins, Honorary Membership Secretary, at the address above
Age range	9–16
Joining fee	none
Annual fee	B but school membership is free
Members	703
Date started	1964

The Crossword Club
Hilberry Farm
Awbridge Hill
Romsey
Hampshire SO51 0HF
Tel: (0794) 513039

The crossword first appeared in England during the nineteenth century. It was very elementary, based upon the word square, and printed in children's puzzle books and various magazines. The Americans first developed the crossword into a serious adult pastime — the first modern puzzle being published in 1913.

The Crossword Club is for those who enjoy tackling really challenging crosswords, and who are prepared to spend time unravelling subtle cryptic clues. When you join The Crossword Club you receive a monthly magazine *Crossword*, which includes two prize crosswords. The first is a difficult *Listener*-type puzzle, almost always involving some kind of gimmick. There is also another competition, either a clue-writing contest, a clue-solving contest or a 'guess the gimmick' competition. Prize winners are awarded book tokens and book plates. Included in the magazine are articles, news and opinions on all aspects of crosswords, especially the construction and solution of the esoteric type of puzzles used in the competition. You have to be quite advanced at crossword puzzles to take part in the competition, but the Club does have some very keen teenage members.

Apply to	the address above
Age range	older readers
Joining fee	none
Annual fee	C
Members	750
Date started	1978

The Heraldry Society

44/45 Museum Street
London WC1A 1LY
Tel: (01) 430 2172 (Mondays, Wednesdays, Thursdays)

This Society exists to encourage interest in heraldry, armory, chivalry and genealogy. It is concerned particularly with helping young enthusiasts.

When you join the Heraldry Society you will receive a copy of *The Heraldry Gazette*, every quarter which includes news, comments, and the Society's programme of activities, as well as a special inset, *Young Armorist*, specially for junior members. You can buy, at special low prices, books and pamphlets published by the Society. There is an excellent library on heraldry, and a growing collection of slides which you can borrow. Meetings are held in London during the winter, and there are exhibitions for you to go to. You can ask the Society for advice and study for the Society's certificate in Elementary, Intermediate and Advanced Heraldry.

Apply to	the Secretary at the address above
Age range	9–16
Joining fee	none
Annual fee	C
Members	1,850
Date started	1950

Military Heraldry Society

c/o 37 Wolsey Close
Southall
Middlesex UB2 4NQ
Tel: (01) 574 4425

If you collect cloth shoulder sleeve insignia this Society gives you the chance to swap information and insignia with other collectors. When you join you will receive a quarterly magazine *Formation Signs*, which gives you information about shoulder titles, regimental and unit flashes, and similar cloth insignia.

Apply to	Lt Cdr W. M. Thornton, at the address above
Age range	older readers
Joining fee	none
Annual fee	B
Members	229
Date started	1951

Esperanto Asocio de Britujo (EAB)

Esperanto Centre
140 Holland Park Avenue
London W11 4UF
Tel: (01) 727 7821

Esperanto is an international language. According to Esperanto Asocio de Britujo (the Esperanto Association of Britain), research has shown that Esperanto is at least five times easier to learn than French, so you can easily hold a conversation in just a few months.

Young people can join the Junularo Esperantista Brita (JEB), and attend regular international youth meetings in many different countries, including seminars, holiday weeks and weekends. There is a penfriend service and free accommodation network, which includes over eight hundred addresses in fifty-three countries if you like travelling abroad.

Apply to	the address above
Age range	older readers
Joining fee	none
Annual fee	C
Members	1,282
Date started	1976

International Language (IDO) Society of Great Britain (ILSGB)

135 Keppoch Street,
Cardiff CF2 3JU
Tel: (0222) 497414

Few of us can speak even one foreign language well, yet in Europe alone there are many languages. An international language should encourage a better understanding between peoples, and Ido is such a language. The vocabulary of Ido is based upon the major European languages and on words taken from Latin. There is no need to learn hundreds of rules and exceptions, irregular verbs, genders, or similar complications, and the words are spelt as they sound. It takes only a fraction of the time to learn Ido as it does for French, German, or Spanish.

Joining this Society is the start of learning Ido. As a member, you receive a twenty-four page newsletter *Ido-Vivo*, written partly in Ido and partly in English, three times a year. Specially for young people the Society has an international youth section, Internaciona Juna Idistaro. If you are interested in knowing more write to the ILSGB.

Apply to	the address above
Age range	older readers
Joining fee	none
Annual fee	A
Members	40
Date started	1913

Friends by Post

6 Bollin Court
Macclesfield Road
Wilmslow
Cheshire SK9 2AP
Tel: (0625) 527044

Friends by Post can choose you a penfriend from either the United Kingdom or the USA. All you have to do is to provide your age and interests. Once you have been given a penfriend, then you should write weekly or fortnightly on Wednesdays. Experience has shown that keeping to a regular posting date is best. You can start your letter in good time, but leave it open to add to as and when you want. You may want to write about what you have heard, seen or read, or about your thoughts and problems. Even everyday happenings, however small, can be of interest, and can make your letters lively and very personal. If writing to your penfriend goes well you can ask for another and increase your circle of friends.

Apply to	Mrs Ilse Salomon, at the address above. Please supply a stamped self-addressed envelope
Age range	older readers
Joining fee	none
Annual fee	none
Members	about 20,000
Date started	1960

Association of Comics Enthusiasts (ACE)

80 Sillerdale
Sydenham
London SE26 4SJ
Tel: (01) 699 7725

This is the first and only club for collectors of British comics and strips. When you join you receive regular copies of a newsletter, *Comic Cuts,* full of current and forthcoming news including reviews of strip books, comic art exhibitions, festivals and conventions, awards and USA visits, as well as members' letters, and plenty of 'Wants and Sales' ads, which include vintage and pre-war items.

The Association has also published thousands of fact-sheets on comics, artists, characters, story-papers, annuals, publishers, free gifts including indexes, chronologies, and stripographies. You get a *Comic Chronology* which lists start and stop dates for juvenile and comic publications in the United Kingdom plus special editions, amalgamations, supplements, and gifts from 1900 to 1939. The intention is eventually to cover the entire history. Another publication is the *A-Z of British Newspaper Strips* which includes one collected example of every strip published. Classic comic heroes, adventure strips and picture serials are featured in special sheets of illustrated information. Annual collectors find the ACE's identification indexes to D.C. Thompson or A.P. invaluable, and the free gift lists are unique, being the first attempt to list and identify these rare collectors' items. Also published in serial form with illustrations are the personal reminiscences of veteran artists who worked in comics, and occasional facsimiles of, for example, the Weary Willie and Tired Tim Club Membership

Certificate, and the leaflets advertising the first issues of *Dandy* and *Beano*. If you take a serious interest in comics and their history this is definitely the Association for you.

Apply to	Mr Denis Gifford, at the address above
Age range	older readers
Joining fee	none
Annual fee	B
Members	180
Date started	1978

British Fantasy Society (BFS)

15 Stanley Road
Morden
Surrey SM4 5DE
Tel: (01) 540 9443

Do you enjoy reading Michael Moorcock, Paul Anderson, Robert Holdstock, Ramsey Campbell, and books such as the *Dune* series, *Mythago Wood, The Damnation Game*; or watching films such as *Gremlins, The Company of Wolves, Mad Max*, and *Back to the Future*? If so, this Society may be just what you are looking for.

When you join the BFS you will receive the *British Fantasy Newsletter*, and a magazine, *Dark Horizons*, which includes articles, fiction, verse, and artwork. The Society also publishes a series of booklets which tell you all about such authors as Michael Moorcock, Ramsey Campbell, Peter Tremayne and William Hope Hodgson.

The BFS also sponsors each year the British Fantasy Convention, Fantasycon, at which you can meet and hear many well-known people from the 'fantasy world', like Gene Wolfe, Charles L. Grant, Ramsey Campbell, Dennis Etchison, Jody Scott and Samantha Lee. At this conference the British Fantasy Awards are announced for the best fantasy novel, story, film, artist and small publisher. There is also a special award which has been given in the past to Manly Wade Wellman, Karl Edward Wagner and Stephen King.

Apply to	Mrs Di Wathen, at the address above
Age range	13–16
Joining fee	none
Annual fee	C
Members	about 270
Date started	1971

British Science Fiction Association (BSFA)

18 Gordon Terrace
Blantyre
Lanarkshire G72 9NA

If you enjoy reading science fiction, then you might like to join the BSFA which encourages the writing, reading and publishing of science fiction, and provides opportunities for SF fans to contact each other and swap views. Founded by a group of authors, readers, publishers and book-sellers of science fiction this Association now has members worldwide, who receive six mailings a year. Included in these mailings are *Matrix*, a newsletter/magazine full of SF news, comment and opinion, reviews, information about local clubs and conventions, and members' letters, *Focus*, published twice a year providing new writers with the chance to write fiction, and swap views and information, and *Paperback Inferno* which reviews all of the latest SF paperbacks.

The BSFA also organises *Orbiter*, a postal workshop for SF writers who can send in their work for an informed opinion, and *Triangle*, another postal workshop this time for SF artists. There is also an information service to answer questions on all aspects of science fiction, a postal magazine chain of the latest SF magazines, and an SF lending library, which is one of the largest in the world.

Apply to	Mr S. Brown, Membership Secretary at the address above
Age range	older readers
Joining fee	none
Annual fee	C
Members	about 2,000
Date started	1958

The Puffin Club

Penguin Books
Bath Road
Harmondsworth
Middlesex UB7 0DA
Tel: (01) 759 5722

This super reading Club keeps you in touch with all that is new and exciting in the world of books. You get a special badge, a membership book, an interesting and colourful twenty-eight page quarterly magazine, *Puffin Post*, full of articles, stories, competitions and news, free entry into London's Great Puffin Carnival and lots of other events organised around Britain, as well as regular offers of books at special low prices.

Apply to	the address above
Age range	9–13
Joining fee	none
Annual fee	B or C for three years. Also free subscription if you select a bookpack for B or C
Members	nearly 30,000
Date started	1967

File of Enemies (FOE)

50 Paynes Meadow
Whitminster
Gloucester GL2 7PS
Tel: (0452) 740785

This is a fully comprehensive central register of anyone interested in any form of game, giving names, addresses, telephone numbers and the games each person prefers. Games include simulation board war-gaming, war-games with miniatures, role-playing, science fiction and fantasy gaming. So, if you want to contact your closest opponent for face-to-face board gaming, weekend campaigns, or role-playing adventures, this register can help you. You never know, you might find that someone in your own street is also on the register and interested in the same games as you!

When you write to FOE you are entered on the register and you are sent details of the six registered members living nearest to you. You receive details of all clubs in your area, and every three months you are informed of all new registrations. Full information on your nearest games' shops and games distributors is also sent to you.

Apply to	Mr Terry Devereux, Administrator, at the address above
Age range	older readers
Joining fee	none
Annual fee	A
Members	1,850
Date started	1979

The Solo War-Gamers' Association (SWA)

50 King Arthur's Road
Exeter
Devon EX4 9BH

War-games with miniatures, board and simulation games, fantasy and role-playing, and computer-assisted war-games are all covered by this Association.

If you join SWA you will receive a magazine, *Lone Warrior*, every two months. There are forty-four pages of articles, letters and comments, reviews and general hobby news. Articles vary from covering the more technical aspects, such as computer applications and probability theory, to advice for beginners on the problems of running solo games. The emphasis is on practical war-gaming. The play-by-mail section of *Lone Warrior* asks questions and gives advice on playing by post. There are also reviews of suitable games and situation reports on games in progress. You can advertise your own individually tailored games or put your name down to play or umpire commercial ones such as Kingmaker or Squad Leader.

SWA also has a small library from which you can borrow, and the exchange of historical and technical information is co-ordinated by the Association.

Apply to	The Membership Secretary, Mr Ian McDowall 50 Stonefield, Bar Hill Cambridge CB3 8TB
Age range	older readers
Joining fee	none
Annual fee	C
Members	500
Date started	1976

The American Civil War Round Table (UK) (ACWRT UK)

98 Kew Green
Kew
Richmond
Surrey TW9 3AP

An interest in the American Civil War often begins when you are young, and people follow this interest for many years unaware that there is an organisation just for them. The ACWRT (UK) is for those who have a genuine interest in the military, naval or civil history of the American Civil War. Does this include you? If so join this Round Table and you will be able to borrow from a library of 150 books, plus magazines, battlefield guides, maps and photographs.

You will receive a quarterly newsletter, *Crossfire*, which includes articles as well as news. Meetings are held four times a year in central London, generally on Saturday evenings. Usually there is a speaker, followed by a question and answer session.

Apply to	the address above
Age range	older readers
Joining fee	none
Annual fee	B
Members	70
Date started	1953

Cross and Cockade International (C and CGB)

Cragg Cottage
The Cragg
Bramham
Wetherby
West Yorkshire LS23 6QB
Tel: (0937) 845320

This is a specialist Society for those with a serious interest in World War I aircraft. Four times a year you will receive a journal which contains factual articles by surviving World War I personnel and some of the world's leading aviation historians. These are

supported by a selection of photographs, many from private collections and very rare. Sometimes accurate scale three-view and three-quarter view cut-away drawings are included. You can go along to meetings held regularly in central London and other parts of the United Kingdom. Details of these and addresses of area secretaries will be sent to you when you join.

Apply to	the Membership Secretary, at the address above
Age range	older readers
Joining fee	none
Annual fee	D
Members	1,220
Date started	1968

British Westerners' Association (BWA)

Camp Farm
Camp Road
Little Hay
Lichfield
Staffordshire
Tel: (021) 308 4573

The BWA is for all those people who are not only interested in Western riding and fast draw shooting, but all the activities which are connected with the American West, past and present.

The interests of BWA members are many and varied: fast draw shooting and Western riding are the most popular, but rope spinning, square dancing, Country & Western music, knife throwing, Western movies, bead and leatherwork and Western cooking are some of the other main activities. There are many members who are very knowledgeable about Western history, while others are expert riders, fast on the draw and good at rifle shooting. There is also a growing interest in the lore and crafts of the American Indian, and many members collect or make their own Western outfits. There are clubs within the Association that concentrate on a particular aspect of life in the West, for example the American Civil War, or the American Indians. Many of the clubs put on shows at fêtes and carnivals to raise money for charity.

As a member you are kept informed about the BWA's activities through a lively, free magazine, *Round-Up* which is sent to you several times a year. There are also Round-Up 'get togethers' held during the year. At these self-catering, camping weekends, you can meet old friends and make new ones, and join in the competitions for which trophies and prizes are awarded.

Apply to	Mr Mark Gaden, at the address above
Age range	9–15 (family membership
Joining fee	none
Annual fee	C (family membership)
Members	over 1,000
Date started	1973

English Westerners' Society (EWS)

29 The Tinings
Monkton Park
Chippenham
Wiltshire SN15 3LY
Tel: (0249) 652177

If you are interested in the American West then you may like to join this Society. As a member you will receive two quarterly publications, *Brand Book* and *Tally Sheet*. The *Brand Book* contains articles, mostly historical and biographical, which are fully documented and based upon original research. The *Tally Sheet*, includes reviews of books, pamphlets and magazines, booklists, Society news, and notes on meetings. You can ask EWS for free information, and will be able to take part in social activities.

Apply to	the address above
Age range	older readers
Joining fee	none
Annual fee	C
Members	300
Date started	1954

More Useful Addresses

Full information on the following organisations was not available at the time of going to press, but will be included in the next edition.

Bicycle Polo Association of Great Britain
72 Upton Road
Haylands
Ryde
Isle of Wight PO33 3HX

Boys' Brigade
Brigade House
Parsons Green
London SW6 4TH

British Chess Federation
9a Grand Parade
St Leonards on Sea
E Sussex TN38 0DD

British Isles Marbles Association
183 Comptons Lane
Horsham
W Sussex

British Kite Fliers Association
PO Box 35
Hemel Hempstead
Herts HP1 1EE

Cetacean Group *(whales and dolphins)*
c/o Zoology Department
University of Oxford
South Parks Road
Oxford OX1 3PS

English Draughts Association
42 Judd Road
Tonbridge TN9 2NH

English Skateboard Association
215 Kensington High Street
London W8

English Tiddlywinks Association
26 Canadian Avenue
London SE6 3AS

Eton Fives Association
Saintbury Close
Saintbury
Nr Broadway
Worcs WR12 7PX

Golf Society of Great Britain
Glen Eagles
Maddox Park
Little Bookham
Surrey KT23 3BW

Model Power Boat Association (UK) Ltd
36 Broadmeads
Ware
Herts

Race Walking Association
1 Rye Hill Flats
Cromwell Hill
Luton
Beds LU1 7PZ

Scottish Chess Association
44 Stewart Clark Avenue
5 Queensferry
Lothian EH30 9QH

MORE USEFUL ADDRESSES

Scottish Wildlife Trust
25 Johnston Terrace
Edinburgh EH1 2NH

Scottish Women's Cross Country & Road Running Association
18 Ainslie Place
Edinburgh EH3 6AU

Shell Collectors Society
3 Acacia Road
Guildford
Surrey

Ship Stamp Society
33a Ridgeway Road
Timperley
Altrincham
Cheshire WA15 7HA

UK Board Sailing Association
30 Rochester Square
London NW1

Vintage Transport Enthusiasts Club
14 Broadway
Lonon SW1

Welsh Chess Union
Iona
Pentwyn Lane
Bettws
Newport NP6 6AF

Woodcraft Folk
13 Ritherdon Road
London SW17

Young Embroiderers Society
Apartment 41a
Hampton Court Palace
East Molesey
Surrey KT8 9AL

If you want to let me know about a club or society which is not mentioned in this book, then cut out this form and send it to me, or copy it out on another sheet of paper. There is space on the back of this form for you to tell me what you like or dislike about the book and what other interests or hobbies you would like to see mentioned.

Your name ______________________________

Your address ______________________________

____

My hobby is ______________________________

I would like to see the following organisation(s) included in the book:

Tick box if you are a member

Name ______________________________ ☐

Address ______________________________

____

Name ______________________________ ☐

Address ______________________________

____

Send to Helen Pain
c/o Northcote House Publishers Ltd
Harper & Row House
Estover Road
Plymouth PL6 7PZ

Use this form to tell me what you think about the book.

I think this book is good because

____

____

____

____

I think this book is not very good because

____

____

____

____

I would like to see more information included in the book on the following hobbies or interests

____

____

____

____

Send to Helen Pain
c/o Northcote House Publishers Ltd
Harper & Row House
Estover Road
Plymouth PL6 7PZ

Index

INDEX

INDEX

INDEX

INDEX